THE
PERCEPTIVE
LEADER

THE
PERCEPTIVE
LEADER

KATHY PEARSON, PHD

and

GREGG PEARSON, PHD

CONTENTS

ACKNOWLEDGEMENTS

Writing a book, even a short tome such as this handbook, is never a solitary endeavor. This project began over two years ago and has progressed through numerous starts and stops. The final product, however, is the result of the work, effort, and talents of many people. It has been an enjoyable undertaking working with a spouse on a project such as this, and a unique collaborative environment with its own challenges too.

First, we would like to give our most gracious thanks to Rosemary Bloser, Managing Partner at ELS. Rosemary has helped to manage the publication of the handbook painstakingly and diligently, with many experiments, obstacles, and opportunities to learn for all of us. Rosemary continues to be a true partner in all endeavors at ELS, including this effort.

We would also like to heartily thank Dr. Stephen Cutcliffe of Lehigh University for a meticulous reading of the entire manuscript. Steve has been a mentor, advisor, colleague, and friend for many years. He is also the most generous golf partner in history. Gregg always has his best rounds when out with Steve. His attention to detail, editing, and suggestions made this handbook a much better product.

Our adult children, Sara and Phil, have on occasion been called upon to weigh in on graphics, cases, and stories. And they have heard, only sometimes, each of us expound on their other parent's quirks and eccentricities. The "kids" have always provided perspective, laughter and love.

Despite the assistance from a truly outstanding team, any errors in this handbook are solely the responsibility of the authors. We hope that you find this book helpful.

INTRODUCTION

Globalization. Digitization. Urbanization. Artificial intelligence, regulations, changing workforce, crowdsourcing, millennials, Generation Z. (Z??? What's after Generation Z???) These are the words, the phrases, the laments we hear from our clients on a regular basis, and the clamor is becoming louder and louder. The business environment has transformed dramatically and exponentially with no end of change in sight. Adding more complexity, while we know change is happening, we often do not know the nature of the change. The U.S. military has coined a phrase for this type of environment, which has gained in popularity across the organizational landscape: VUCA (Volatility, Uncertainty, Complexity, Ambiguity).

Consider, for example, the delivery of healthcare in the U.S. With the passing of the Affordable Care Act, or Obamacare, the reimbursement model for hospitals and individual providers changed dramatically. Without delving into the politics, the reality was that some players were happy about the changes and some, not so much. But at least the change was a *known known* (to steal a phrase from Donald Rumsfeld). And then on November 8, 2016—Election Day in the U.S.—that reimbursement model immediately came under threat. A group of senior leaders from a large health system met on the Friday after the election. Of the 20 people in the room, their individual voting choices may well have mirrored the voting pattern of the American population. But from a strategic perspective, every single person in that room was in deep shock. Not only did they know the reimbursement model for healthcare delivery was, likely, going to change (with a Republican President and Republican House and Senate on the legislative side), but they had no idea *how* it would change. Imagine not knowing how you will be paid for services four years from now! And the uncertainty is not abating. As this handbook goes to press, the political and judicial landscape is shifting once again for these health care leaders, and it is nearly impossible to predict with accuracy the health care model or environment in the future.

With this chaos, how does an organization meet its short-term goals while anticipating and preparing for the unknown future? We are convinced that organizations and their leaders need to build the capability to be more **Perceptive**, or more "insightful, discerning, observant" (a few of the synonyms offered by thesaurus.com for "perceptive"). In short, Perceptive Leaders understand they cannot predict the future with accuracy, but still must be able to operate proactively in this environment of change. They know they need to develop the ability to become more discerning and observant to anticipate early indicators of change, not lagging indicators. This handbook provides ten core capabilities to thrive in a VUCA environment. We have created the acronym, PERCEPTIVE, to represent these capabilities, with ten corresponding chapters.

How have we determined this list of ten capabilities? And aren't there many, many books already written about this topic of "Managing Uncertainty"? Certainly, we are not offering new research in the areas of decision making or strategy or strategic execution. So, what is the basis for our work?

First, we draw from established scholarly research (where it is truly applied research, not theory) and anecdotal evidence based on many years working with and in organizations. Consider the work of Dan Lovallo and Olivier Sibony, management professors and researchers. They conducted interesting research on strategic outcomes in a study on *behavioral strategy*. The researchers conclude that there are three major factors that determine an outcome of a major decision—uncertainties, the quality of the decision process, and the use of analytics. Annie Duke makes the same argument in her anecdotal experience as a professional poker player. Duke argues that outcomes depend upon luck (uncertainty) but also the player's skill. These concepts and others have led to the conclusion that Perceptive Leaders must both improve their decision making skills and learn to manage uncertainty in order to achieve better strategic outcomes.

Many of us remember the infamous New Coke decision, with clearly a negative outcome. Was there a lack of strong decision making skills? Or did the Coca-Cola leaders just neglect to manage uncertainty effectively? Without elaborating, the casual observer knows that Coke did not consider the strength of the brand and brand loyalty—clearly a flaw in the decision making process. And Coke also chose to eliminate the original Coke when introducing New Coke, a lapse in managing the risk or uncertainty adequately.

Second, we share real world lessons from two different perspectives. Each chapter provides best practices in behaviors and capabilities, based on Kathy's interactions with senior leaders across industries and regions of the world. We also draw from Gregg's vast expertise and knowledge in the fields of leadership, the corporate environment, history and the military. Finally, we reference experts from actual organizations and professions.

To communicate this work, we have organized the handbook chapters to provide insight in three areas:

- A description of the capability with supporting research and anecdotes on its correlation to good performance, prepared by Kathy.

- Key leadership behaviors to build the capability within organizations.

- A detailed case study illustrating the capability, either in a military setting or in a commercial venture, developed and written by Gregg.

Why did we decide to call this manuscript a *handbook* for leaders? We knew we wanted to provide *practical, useful, and actionable* advice for leaders. We also wanted supporting and reinforcing material to complement our work with executives in the classroom and in leadership teams. We wanted to bring these lessons alive through real stories and lessons from the past. The word handbook? Gregg thought about his Ranger Handbook from his days as an infantry officer and Airborne Ranger. He kept that hand book close at hand, hence, it was a hand book, throughout his military career because it was concrete and actionable, and the information was easily accessible. We hope that you find the lessons in this handbook concrete and actionable as well.

One final note: the reader will notice two very different styles of writing in each chapter. Kathy's style is fairly informal and even conversational in parts. Gregg, on the other hand, writes like a true historian, including detail and analysis. For the sake of our marriage, we decided that we would not try to blend our styles (this last sentence was written by Kathy, for example). We hope you enjoy our two voices!

CHAPTER ONE

Purpose

If you cannot explain it simply, you don't understand it well enough.

–Albert Einstein, scientist

The Concept

Having true clarity of **Purpose** is a foundational characteristic of a Perceptive Leader. So often, if employees are asked to articulate the overall strategic intent of their organization, they will either give a generic answer such as "create profits for our shareholders" or shrug their shoulders in ignorance. The military explicitly addresses the need for clarity of purpose in its demand for a clear "commander's intent" for every mission. When heading into battle, for example, even the lowest ranking foot soldier must understand the overall goal of the commander.

Why is clarity of purpose so important in the military (and in organizations)?

- We all know that to achieve high performance, a leader must motivate and inspire his or her team members.

- One of the core themes of this handbook is the need for *adaptability in an uncertain environment.* Soldiers and employees cannot adapt easily if they do not understand the strategic intent. Adaptability and agility are key elements in managing uncertainty and are addressed at length in subsequent chapters.

- A well-articulated and communicated purpose or strategic intent becomes a powerful tool in prioritizing resources and efforts.

Research certainly supports this need for clarity. For example, Larry Hrebiniak, professor of management, in his book *Making Strategy Work*, presents the results of two surveys of executives on the obstacles to strategic execution. In both surveys, "poor or vague strategy" was listed as one of the primary barriers, implying lack of clarity. Researchers Donald Sull, Rebecca Homkes, and Charles Sull report in the *Harvard Business Review* that senior leaders place great emphasis on frequent communication of their strategy to ensure successful execution. Yet, their research illustrates that clarity of the strategy is much more elusive. While 84% of employees reported that the strategy was clear, less than one third could accurately articulate the top priorities.

Of course, this idea of clarity of purpose is easy to articulate in a handbook but a bit harder to put into practice. Recently the US Army War College designed an executive development program for newly-minted two-star general officers with Wharton Executive Education. Kathy was honored to participate in this endeavor. When she discussed the concept of commander's intent with these senior military leaders, she humbly said, "I'm embarrassed to even present this concept to you! So many of our principles in management and management science have roots in military leadership and training." One of the general officers replied, "We are very good at providing the commander's intent in the battlefield. But as soon as we get back to garrison, we seem to completely forget that lesson!" He articulated the difficulty in providing clarity of purpose in a complex, sometimes bureaucratic organization.

What Should I Do as a Perceptive Leader to Achieve Clarity of Purpose?

- When considering a major decision or strategic initiative, ensure everyone on the leadership team or project team understands and *agrees* with the overall purpose.

- State the purpose explicitly in one or two sentences such that someone else who did not participate in the discussions can understand the purpose or intent.

- Test the articulation of the purpose with a diverse set of employees within the organization. Is it clear and consistent? Does it provide the overall guidance that every echelon needs to be successful?

Case Study

The 2nd Ranger Battalion on D-Day—June 6, 1944

Key Points

- A group of Rangers involved in the US invasion of Normandy on D-Day were given a very clear commander's intent from their commander, Colonel Rudder, for their mission that day: Capture or destroy key German artillery units.

- Colonel Rudder made certain that every member of his unit understood his intent.

- There were setbacks in timing, weather, malfunctioning equipment, and displacement of their objectives. However, the commander's plan was not aborted, merely adjusted.

- The three individual Rangers who accomplished the mission were lower-level supervisors, so they were not involved in planning the mission. However, their individual initiative and complete understanding of Rudder's intent led to a successful completion of the unit's assigned task.

The Story

Point-du-Hoc is located along the Normandy coast in France and was the scene of one of the most daring and audacious feats of arms by American Forces on D-Day. The promontory was situated between the two American landing beaches—Omaha and Utah. The specific position was 7 kilometers from the center of Omaha and 20 kilometers from Utah. Point-du-Hoc was so named because it sits atop 40 meter cliffs of clay and access to it was only thought possible from the land—a seaborne landing was viewed as impossible by the Germans. Additionally, Point-du-Hoc was the highest point between Omaha and Utah and held a commanding view of the entire American landing area. The Germans recognized the importance of the location and made it a key independent fortress in their Atlantic Wall defenses. Tons of

Point-du-Hoc in the distance, as viewed from Omaha Beach.

reinforced concrete were used to make fortified trenches, shelters for their soldiers, and casements for a battery of six 155mm artillery pieces. These guns could range both Utah and Omaha beaches, as well as wreak havoc on Allied shipping adjacent to the beaches. The capture of these heights was paramount for the success of the Allied landings on D-Day.

The cliffs at Point-du-Hoc.

The mission to capture the German artillery battery at Point-du-Hoc was assigned to the 2nd Ranger Battalion. The Ranger force was commanded by Colonel James Earl Rudder, a legendary figure in the history of the Rangers. He outlined two specific missions for the force attacking Point-du-Hoc. First, capture or destroy the German 155mm guns. Second, cut the hard-surface coast road, known as the Vierville Road, connecting Utah and Omaha to prevent German reinforcements from arriving at the beaches. Colonel Rudder's plan assigned specific casements, enemy artillery pieces and trenches, to each unit. Every soldier knew precisely his individual unit assignment. Rudder also made certain that everyone in the unit understood the overall intent of the mission—capture or destroy the guns. Conducting the Ranger mission were three companies, D, E, and F, of the 2nd Ranger Battalion. This force consisted of only 225 soldiers, but they were well-trained prior to the invasion. Their training in the Highlands of Scotland consisted of long speed-marches to improve their fitness, obstacle courses for strength and dexterity, hand-to-hand combat skills for close encounters with the enemy, and mountaineering with an emphasis on cliff climbing using specialized equipment. The Ranger advantages of stealth, physical fitness, individual initiative, and tenacity were designed to overcome their small numbers and light armament.

Colonel James Earl Rudder.

The 2nd Ranger Battalion was the beneficiary of several pre-invasion preparations. First, aerial reconnaissance gave them the information required to develop their detailed plans. Second, aerial bombardment by American and British forces of Point-du-Hoc was designed to destroy the German gun emplacements and defenses, thereby making the Ranger mission less risky. Finally, naval gunfire from the *USS Texas* and her ten 14-inch guns was to commence 30 minutes before the Rangers landed at the base of the cliffs. The naval gunfire was calculated to destroy the German force providing security and support for the 155mm battery. Altogether, Point-du-Hoc was hit by more than ten kilotons of high explosives prior to the Ranger landings, a force equivalent to the atomic bomb used at Hiroshima. Contemporary visitors can still view the moonscape terrain atop the cliffs of Point-du-Hoc.

The plateau above the cliffs of Point-du-Hoc. The craters
are from the pre-invasion bombardment.

The 2nd Ranger Battalion was scheduled to land at the base of the cliffs at 0630 on June 6, 1944, but they encountered several problems. The tidal surge in the English Channel pushed them well off course, thereby delaying their landing until 0710—a critical 40 minutes in which the enemy had an opportunity to recover. The stormy weather in the Channel created waves which swamped their ten landing craft and four DUKWs (an amphibious craft that could also traverse land) soaking the men and their equipment. The aerial and naval bombardment caused chunks of the cliffs to tumble down upon the narrow beach, which was quickly disappearing due to the rising tide. Finally, their specialized climbing equipment, ladders from the London

Fire Department and pneumatic launch tubes for their grapnel hooks, was wet and malfunctioned. The Rangers would have to scale the 40 meter high cliffs using old-fashioned methods—hand ropes and rope ladders—all the while facing enemy fire from above the cliffs. Nevertheless, the Rangers began their assault at 0710 and were atop the cliffs in force by 0730.

On the plateau above the cliffs, the Rangers encountered sporadic German resistance, which they quickly overcame. The Germans had not expected an assault from the sea, so most of their defenses were pointed toward the landward approaches to Point-du-Hoc. However, the Ranger mission and commander's intent was not to kill Germans, but to destroy the guns. The Rangers were quite dismayed to discover that the German artillery battery was gone. Units assigned to destroy specific gun casements quickly realized their objectives were empty. The Rangers then transitioned to their secondary mission and bisected the Vierville Road, established a strong defensive position, set-up roadblocks, and sent out patrols in search of the German guns, all by 0815 or roughly 45 minutes after they landed at the base of the cliffs.

Remnants of a German gun casement at Point-du-Hoc.

One of the patrols, led by Staff Sergeant Leonard Lomell and Sergeant Jack Kuhn, discovered a dirt road leading inland. Lomell and Kuhn were non-commissioned officers, the backbone of the Army, and in business terms were first-line supervisors. The dirt road had heavy tracks in it, so they investigated further. About a kilometer inland, Lomell and Kuhn discovered the German guns. They were well-camouflaged and pointed in the direction of Utah Beach. The German unit assigned to the guns was located in shelters a few hundred meters from the guns but were forming up to man the weapons. The German battery had evidently been pulled back from their positions on the plateau at Point-du-Hoc for fear of being destroyed during the pre-invasion bombardment. Without hesitation, Lomell and Kuhn, working together, smashed the siting mechanism on one of the guns, and disabled two other guns by using thermite grenades to melt their recoil and traversing mechanisms. However, three of the artillery pieces were still functional. Lomell and Kuhn raced back to American lines, collected more thermite grenades, and eventually destroyed the other three guns. At nearly the same time as Lomell and Kuhn were destroying the German guns, a patrol under the command of Sergeant Frank Rupinski discovered the ammunition dump which supplied the battery. Using plastic explosives, Rupinski and his Rangers detonated the German shells.

The bottom line was that by 0900 on June 6, 1944, the 2nd Ranger Battalion had accomplished its missions of destroying the German artillery battery and bisecting the coastal road. It was the first, and one of the few, American units to completely accomplish their mission on D-Day. The 2nd Ranger Battalion at Point-du-Hoc was neither resupplied nor reinforced until June 9. At the end of the three-day battle, there were only 90 of the initial 225 Rangers who were not killed or wounded.

There are two key learning points from the story of the 2nd Ranger Battalion on D-Day. First, Colonel Rudder made certain that every member of his unit understood his intent—capture or destroy the German artillery atop Point-du-Hoc. Despite setbacks in timing, weather, malfunctioning equipment, and displacement of their objectives, his plan was not aborted, merely adjusted. By adhering to the intent of their mission, and not becoming a victim of unfavorable circumstances, the Rangers accomplished their mission. Secondly, commander's intent needs to be understood and impressed upon every member of an organization. It is telling that the individual Rangers who accomplished the mission—Lomell, Kuhn, and Rupinski—were not involved in planning the mission, a charge normally left to officers, as they were lower-level supervisors. However, their individual initiative and complete understanding of Rudder's intent were absolutely critical in accomplishing the unit's assigned task. Commander's intent MUST permeate every echelon of an organization to be successful.

CHAPTER TWO

Experiential Frames

Good leadership requires you to surround yourself with people of diverse perspectives who can disagree with you without fear of retaliation.

–Doris Kearns Goodwin, historian and author

The Concept

In the field of critical thinking, we often discuss the effects of our own **Experiential Frames**. Humans tend to subconsciously assess any situation, person, or decision in the context of our previous experiences. Every individual builds a view of the world based on historical experiences over time. Three challenges exist with these experiential frames:

- When faced with challenging situations or decisions, no one person possesses the depth and breadth of experiences that could be relevant to solving a problem or making a decision.

- As the external conditions change, prior experiences may no longer be relevant to the situation.

- Humans are naturally biased, both as part of the human condition and individually.

We cannot eliminate this natural tendency to rely on our past experiences, nor can we change our instinctive resistance to change, but we can put practices in place to mitigate these effects. Specifically, Perceptive Leaders seek diversity of thought.

Before continuing the discussion on experiential frames and the need for diversity of thought, let's pause for a moment to introduce the field of behavioral economics. Many of the concepts developed in this field are relevant to decision making and managing uncertainty effectively. In the early 1970s, two cognitive psychologists—Daniel Kahneman and Amos Tversky—became quite interested in the seeming irrationality of humans in decision making. They identified patterns and found that there were many different types of predictable biases that can lead to irrational decision making behaviors. (As of 2019 there were 193 biases listed on the "cognitive biases" Wikipedia page.) Tversky passed away in 1996, but Kahneman won the Nobel Prize in Economics in

2002 for one of their theories known as prospect theory, which we will explore later. In fact, throughout this handbook, there will be references not only to prospect theory but also to some of the most important cognitive biases that hinder Perceptive Leadership.

Returning to our discussion on experiential frames, prospect theory is quite relevant. A manifestation of experiential frames is the very familiar resistance-to-change mantra, "But we have always done it this way!", especially when "this way" has been successful in the past. Our historical database of experiences tells us that "this way" is a good way. And prospect theory makes the case that humans are not interested in taking risks when something has worked well. Specifically, prospect theory demonstrates that humans are very risk averse with gains, but more risk taking with losses (we will try to avoid a loss at all costs!). This cognitive bias is the psychological reason why people naturally do not like change. How many times have employees said "Why are we changing the process / product / structure / incentive plan? If it ain't broke, don't fix it!" In fact, most change management models include the imperative to create a sense of urgency to highlight potential loss.

Experiential frames and our aversion to change are two of the reasons decision scientists encourage diversity of thought when making group decisions. A plethora of studies exist that demonstrate decisions made by heterogeneous groups are of higher quality than homogeneous groups. We provide several examples here that we think are indicative of the body of research and have practical applications for Perceptive Leaders. These studies show that diverse teams lead to improved performance and financial success.

In 2017, Boston Consulting Group studied 1700 companies from a variety of industries of different size across multiple countries to determine the impact of diversity. The researchers defined diversity within the management teams along six dimensions: gender, age, country of origin, career path, industry background, and educational focus. The research design was quite robust in terms of methods and variables, and discovered two important findings. First, companies with "above average" diverse management teams experienced profit margins nine percentage points higher than the less diverse management teams.

Secondly, companies with more diverse management teams had 19 percent higher revenue directly attributed to innovation.

Another study on diversity of thought, conducted by researcher Brian Uzzi, examined the optimal mix of team members developing Broadway plays. He developed a metric that he refers to as a "Q score" that captured the familiarity of team members prior to their work together. His research found that the teams that contained some members who had common past experiences, but also had "newcomers," developed the most successful Broadway plays. In other words, teams with some folks who have shared experiences but that also allow fresh ideas and perspectives are the most efficient and effective.

Finally, in 2017, professors of strategy Allison Lewis and David Reynolds introduced the concept of cognitive diversity, which they define as "differences in perspectives or information processing style." Their study on performance in formulating and executing a strategy in an executive simulation exercise has implications for the Perceptive Leader and a Perceptive Organization. Their research found little correlation between success in the simulated exercise and the more traditional types of diversity: age, ethnicity, and gender. However, using a measurement of cognitive diversity developed by Peter Robinson that he calls the "AEM-Cube," Lewis and Reynolds discovered a high positive correlation between the level of cognitive diversity and success in the exercise.

In summary, Perceptive Leaders understand that individual experiential frames are innate, but research and experience demonstrate that they can overcome the negative impact of experiential frames by seeking diversity of thought. And as a bit of foreshadowing, organizations as well as individuals exhibit this same tendency to build an experiential frame of their environment based on their experiences in the past. Author Jim Collins, in his book *Great by Choice*, calls this ability to challenge the organizational experiential frame "Productive Paranoia," which has become one of our favorite phrases and is the subject of Chapter Six in this handbook.

What Should I Do as a Perceptive Leader to Understand My Experiential Frame and to Build Diversity of Thought on My Teams?

- Analyze your own experiences as they relate to your role as leader. Do you have a preponderance of experiences in dealing with colleagues or direct reports that could influence your view? Have you challenged the underlying assumptions?

- Seek the opinions of employees and colleagues who have different experiences than you, not only in ethnicity, age or gender, but also in cognitive diversity areas such as perspective and knowledge processing.

- Most organizations today have "diversity and inclusion" personnel on staff. Explore these resources within your organization to help promote diversity of thought, and promote cognitive diversity in the diversity and inclusion effort.

Case Study

Abraham Lincoln and the American Civil War

Key Points

- Abraham Lincoln helped form a new party, The Republican Party, on the basis of halting the expansion of slavery.

- Lincoln had many opponents in his presidential bid in 1860, with many differing opinions and policies.

- Lincoln won the election for President in a time of great national dysfunction and crisis. He knew his most important task was to bring the Union together.

- Lincoln chose to develop a strong coalition across the fractured parties by building a diverse cabinet of leaders, many of whom were political opponents.

- Lincoln also knew that by selecting a cabinet of diverse thinkers, he would be served well in the many difficult decisions that he would face in his presidency.

The Story

... we heard the result [Lincoln's election in 1860] *coldly
and sadly. It seemed too rash, on a purely local reputation,
to build so grave a trust in such anxious times.*

–Ralph Waldo Emerson

Arguably, the 1850s were the most tumultuous decade in the history
of the United States. The country was fracturing over the issue
of slavery. In the 1840s America had conquered much of the west
and southwest upon the conclusion of the Mexican-American War in
1848. The political question of the time was whether slavery would be
introduced and extended into these new territories. The debate over
slavery included the Compromise of 1850, the Fugitive Slave Law, the
Kansas-Nebraska Act, the *Dred Scott* case in 1857, and the ideology of
popular sovereignty where the citizens of a territory would vote whether
they wanted slavery to exist within their new state.

Into this maelstrom of political discourse, the new Republican Party
emerged in the mid-1850s. The bedrock belief of the Republicans was
to oppose the extension of slavery into new territories or states where it
currently did not exist. They believed that this was the proper course of
action towards the eventual eradication of the institution. The Republican
Party nominated its first candidate for president in 1856, John C.
Fremont, a celebrated explorer and hero of the Mexican-American War.
The Party was establishing new branches in most non-slave states, and
in Illinois one of its early members was Abraham Lincoln.

Lincoln was born in 1809 into a poor Kentucky family. His family
eventually emigrated west and settled in Illinois. Lincoln did not receive
much, if any, formal education and was self-taught. He studied law,
became a lawyer and practiced by "riding the circuit" in central Illinois.
He established a law practice in Springfield, Illinois with partner

William Herndon. During his time in Springfield, Lincoln became a leader in the Whig Party and served as a state representative for eight years and later a single two-year term as a representative in Congress. Lincoln ran twice for the United States Senate, losing both times. His 1858 defeat to Democrat Stephen A. Douglas is what gained Lincoln a national following. The famed Lincoln-Douglas Debates demonstrated that he was intelligent and also an outstanding orator—a critical skill for nineteenth-century politicians. Lincoln was an opponent of slavery extension under any conditions and abhorred the inhumanity of the institution.

Lincoln demonstrated other skills during his Senate campaigns which would serve him well as a national leader. In addition to his intelligence, he had an uncanny ability to grasp the complexity of problems—he saw the "big picture." He had a homespun sense of humor. When once asked about his experience fighting in the Black Hawk War in the 1830s along the Illinois-Iowa border, Lincoln replied that "the only thing I fought was mosquitos." Lincoln's decency, sensitivity, compassion, honesty, and empathy were highly regarded by friends and foes alike. In short, he had a strong moral character and the ambition to perform great works for the benefit of others.

1860 Republican Convention and General Election

Abraham Lincoln's national reputation had risen enough by 1860 for him to be considered a candidate for the Republican Party nomination for president. Albeit a longshot, with little support outside of Illinois, Lincoln and his team began their quest. The 1860 Republican Convention was held in the booming metropolis of Chicago in mid-May. In order to attract more general support, the new party expanded its platform to include issues important to fringe parties. The Republicans called for a Homestead Act to award free government land to western settlers. They also proposed an import tariff to protect certain industries and a transcontinental railroad to attract west coast backing. One very significant procedural decision at the convention was that a simple majority was all that was needed to win the nomination, as opposed to a two-thirds majority, as had been the case in 1856. There were 465 delegates to the convention, so 233 would be needed to win.

Lincoln faced several challengers for the nomination. Most famous of these, and the leading candidate, was William A. Seward of New York. Seward was considered too conservative on slavery and too liberal on immigration issues by many delegates, especially in the states of Illinois, Indiana, New Jersey, and Pennsylvania. He also had many political enemies, and some delegates saw him as incapable of winning the general election. The other leading challengers were Salmon Chase of Ohio, a strong anti-slavery politician, and Edward Bates of Missouri, a moderate. Lincoln, being a realist, believed that his support was strong only in Illinois, so he endeavored to be the second choice of most, if not all, of the assembled delegates. His team worked tirelessly to convince the convention that Lincoln was a compromise candidate to Seward. Their strategy worked. On the first ballot, the tally was Seward 173½, Lincoln 102, Chase 49, and Bates 48. By the second ballot, Seward gained minimal ground and finished with 184½ votes to Lincoln's 181. The candidacies of Chase and Bates had lost momentum. On the third ballot, Lincoln finished with 235½ votes, with critical support from former Chase and Bates delegates, and thereby won the nomination.

The 1860 general election presented the Republicans with a distinct problem. They were still much smaller than the Democratic Party, and they had little appeal outside the North. The seminal event of this election was the fracturing of the Democratic Party into two distinctive parts: Northern Democrats and Southern Democrats. The issue was, of course, slavery. The Northern Democrats desired some minor prohibitions on the institution, while the Southern Democrats wanted slavery to expand into the territories. The Democrats held two conventions in 1860 and fielded two candidates. John C. Breckenridge of Kentucky secured the nomination for the Southern Democrats, while Lincoln's old Illinois nemesis, Stephen A. Douglas, won the Northern Democrats' nomination. There was also a fourth party in 1860—The Constitutional Union Party. The platform of the Constitutional Unionists was to avoid secession over slavery. Their platform had three points—support the Constitution, maintain the Union, and enforce all existing laws. The candidate of this short-lived party was John Bell of Tennessee. Lincoln won the election with a plurality of the popular vote, 39.8%, but a majority of the electoral vote with a total of 180. He won eighteen states. Breckenridge won 72 electoral votes, 18.1% of the popular vote, and eleven states. Bell and Douglas finished with 39 and 12 electoral votes, respectively. Bell won Virginia, Kentucky, and Tennessee. Douglas only won Missouri, but still garnered 29.5% of the popular vote. He would eventually become a great supporter of President Lincoln.

President-elect Lincoln had several immediate tasks upon winning the election. Underlying these tasks was his belief that the institution of slavery must not expand beyond where it was already practiced. First, he needed to keep the Union together. This was an almost impossible task as seven states of the eventual Confederate States of America seceded before he was inaugurated in March 1861, based upon a pre-election promise to do so if he were elected. However, there were some pockets of Unionist sentiment in several of the seceding states and slave-holding states that had yet to secede. He needed to keep these states as members of the Union and support southern Unionists. Second, he needed to politically unite the North behind him. This required the support of key Democratic Party leaders. His initial action was to appoint several Democrats as general officers, such as George McClellan, Nathaniel Banks, and Benjamin Butler. The record of these political-generals would be mixed, especially that of McClellan, but appointing them was an act of political expediency. Finally, Lincoln had to form a cabinet in order to govern. His impulse, again, was to gain support and legitimacy by gathering together political rivals, who came with a diverse range of thought, and form them into a team.

Selection of the Cabinet

Lincoln sought to form his cabinet from all factions of the Republican Party and also gain representation from outside of it. He had dual purposes. First, Lincoln wanted to gain consensus and unity on as wide a base as possible in the North. This required a Cabinet with different political experiences than Lincoln, and geographic representation outside of Illinois. Secondly, he wanted diversity of thought in his principal advisors, which he assured through his initial appointments.

Lincoln first turned to his adversaries for the Republican nomination and offered them cabinet posts. Traditionally, a leading figure of the winning party was offered the post of Secretary of State. Lincoln made the offer to William Seward. He was a former governor and senator from New York and had supported Lincoln in the general election and delivered the state. He was a strong supporter of Lincoln and union, yet often sought compromise with southern states. Seward was one of only two initial cabinet members to serve Lincoln until 1865. Salmon Chase was offered the post of Secretary of the Treasury. The former Ohio governor was a Radical Republican and from the faction of the party which wanted immediate abolition and sought no compromise with the South on secession. Chase would later leave this post in 1864 and become Chief Justice of the Supreme Court. Edward Bates from Missouri was Lincoln's choice as Attorney General. Bates was a moderate Republican, like Lincoln, but he came from the critical western state of Missouri, which was already a battleground state on the slavery issue. These three men had been his primary opponents for the nomination in May 1860, and they represented the extremes and center of Republican ideology.

The two other Republicans to whom Lincoln offered cabinet posts were Simon Cameron of Pennsylvania and Caleb Smith of Indiana. Cameron was Lincoln's initial choice for Secretary of War, while Smith was selected as Secretary of the Interior. Both Cameron and Smith had been instrumental in delivering their respective states to Lincoln in the general election, so Lincoln sought to reward them with cabinet posts. Cameron was the first member of the cabinet to resign, in early 1862, over charges of disorganization and corruption.

Lincoln also enlisted the support of current and former Democratic Party officials in his cabinet. After Cameron resigned in early 1862, he was replaced by Edwin Stanton. He came strongly recommended by both Seward and Chase for the post and had also been the Attorney General under Lincoln's predecessor, President James Buchanan. Stanton began the war as a Democrat, but switched party affiliations in 1862. He proved to be extremely adept during the course of the conflict in organizing Northern resources. Democrat Montgomery Blair came from an extremely influential political family in Maryland. As Postmaster General, the former lawyer also switched party affiliations during the war, but rejoined the Democratic Party after the War. He took a firm stance with the southern states and balanced some of the more conciliatory members of the cabinet. The final member to join Lincoln's cabinet was Gideon Welles as Secretary of the Navy. Welles was a Connecticut Democrat, who eventually switched party affiliations too. Lincoln wanted his Secretary of the Navy to come from a maritime state. Welles was a very capable leader of the Navy, strong supporter of Lincoln, and stayed at this post until after the cessation of hostilities in 1865.

Lincoln and his Cabinet at the first reading
of the Emancipation Proclamation in 1862.

Abraham Lincoln arguably assembled one of the most diverse Cabinets in American political history. His Cabinet contained Republicans and Democrats representing nearly the entire spectrum of Northern political thought. His members represented national geographic diversity, excepting the South, and these regions all had differing political views and interests. The diverse political experience of his Cabinet—including several former state governors—dwarfed Lincoln's limited national experience. His Cabinet provided Abraham Lincoln a reservoir of diverse political thought, geographic focus, and political experience which served him well in making the crucial decisions of his presidency and the Civil War.

CHAPTER THREE

Range of Alternatives

It ain't what you don't know that gets you into trouble.
It's what you know for sure that just ain't so.

–Mark Twain, author and humorist

The Concept

In any decision model we have encountered in application or theory, the model includes a phase focused on "developing and evaluating alternatives." Many tools exist to assist the decision maker in analysis and evaluation. Particularly with complex situations, however, people often develop a limited set of options rather than considering a wider **Range of Alternatives**.

This tendency is partially caused by our experiential frames, discussed in the last chapter. Reframing is one tool to use to view a decision with a new perspective. As an example, the CEO of a major apparel company explained his enlightenment regarding the marketplace as a result of reframing his thinking. His company concentrates on the luxury market across a spectrum of apparel categories. When he first joined the organization, he wanted to learn more about the target client. He obtained permission to view a sampling of luxury clients' clothing closets. There, the CEO saw many high fashion brands, but also many mass apparel brands (such as brands sold in mid-market stores), even though these clients could afford an entire closet of high end clothes. He remarked later, "I thought we wanted to gain more customers in the luxury market to increase market share, but I realized we just needed to concentrate on gaining a greater percentage of the closet!"

Another reason people often limit the number of alternatives to consider is the manifestation of the overconfidence bias, studied extensively in behavioral economics. As humans, we are not very good at understanding what we do *not* know, or realizing the depth of our ignorance on a subject. This bias can overtly be seen in forecasting and predictions, but also in evaluating problems and alternatives. For example, former BP CEO Tony Hayward not only exhibited overconfidence in his ability to evaluate the Deepwater Horizon environmental damage, but initially explored a limited set of options in stopping the oil spill. In May 2010 Hayward was quoted as saying, "The Gulf of Mexico is a very big ocean. The amount of volume of oil and dispersant we are putting into it is tiny in relation to the total water volume." In addressing the looming environment disaster (that he had underestimated), Hayward limited his options to a siphon that was inserted into one of the ruined pipes on May 17 and even declared, "I do feel that we have, for the first time, turned the corner in this challenge." The oil spill was not completely sealed until September 19th, four months after Hayward's statement.

Brothers and authors Chip and Dan Heath in their book, *Decisive: How to Make Better Choices in Life and Work,*" share research conducted by Paul Nutt in 1993. Nutt examined 168 decisions made by senior leaders across organizations and found that only 29 percent considered more than one alternative. To address this problem, the brothers present a technique called "multi-tracking" to generate a wider range of options. Multi-tracking uses teams of people with varied backgrounds to simultaneously develop multiple solutions to a problem or alternatives to a decision. Each team examines the problem from a specific frame, such as a particular functional area (operations, sales, finance), a particular area of root causes (people, process, culture), or a particular scope (broad, strategic, detailed, tactical).

Of course, in reality the number of new and creative alternatives to complex situations is infinite, leading to a potential problem in seeking *too many* options. There is no magic number or algorithm for the optimal number of alternatives. At some point a team must actually make a choice and move towards implementation. We suggest a disciplined approach to reaching a conclusion that often is referred to as *decision rights* or *decision governance.* To establish decision rights for unstructured problems, the team should determine the following:

- Who will make the final decision? Some organizations call this "assigning the D."

- When will the decision be made? This criterion ensures the team does not fall into the trap of "getting one more set of data" or "developing one more creative alternative."

These criteria should be determined early in the decision making process and allow for time to generate a creative set of options, as well as a period to evaluate those options, but still enforce an endpoint.

In summary, Perceptive Leaders take the time to develop a broad set of alternatives, but also have the discipline to make a final decision.

What Should I Do as a PERCEPTIVE Leader to Develop a Range of Alternatives When Deciding?

- Reframe the problem from another perspective or angle.

- Use the "multi-tracking" technique where 3-4 disparate teams from different backgrounds develop sets of alternatives.

- Establish firm decision rights, particularly a specific date for the final decision to be made.

Case Study

The Current War

Key Points

- In the late nineteenth century, there was a major battle for dominance between two different currents for a nationwide electric grid system.

- Thomas Edison had extensive experience in electricity innovation and developed a particular point of view about currents based on his prior work.

- Even when presented with potential problems with direct current (expensive with long distance challenges), and with fresh, independent ideas, such as alternating current from Nikola Tesla, Edison would not entertain other alternatives when considering how to build a national grid system.

- Edison's experiential frames of the past as well as his overconfidence bias narrowed his range of alternatives for the future.

The Story

The late nineteenth century was the era in which electricity began to supplant water and steam power as the motive energy force in America. It was also a time in which new electrical inventions mesmerized the American public and imbued them with a sense of wonder, amazement, and excitement for future progress. There are two types of electrical current—direct current and alternating current. Direct current (DC) is the unidirectional flow or movement of electric charge carriers (which are usually electrons). The intensity of the current can vary with time and distance, but the general direction of movement stays the same at all times. The voltage in direct current is relatively low and safe to handle and there are fewer pulsations—highs and lows—in the current flow. Alternating current (AC) occurs when charge carriers in a conductor or semiconductor periodically reverse their direction of movement. The voltage of an AC power source can be easily changed by means of a power transformer. This allows the voltage to be stepped up (increased) for transmission and distribution. High-voltage transmission is more efficient than low-voltage transmission over long distances, because the loss caused by conductor resistance decreases as the voltage increases. In other words, AC is very efficient for long-distance transmission, but the high-voltage must be converted into safe voltage ranges for use in households through a transformer.

In the 1880s and 1890s a battle raged throughout America on which type of current should be the basis for an American electrical power grid. Thomas Edison was the key proponent of DC, while Serbian-American Nikola Tesla was the inventor of an AC transmission system. Tesla's primary financial backer was George Westinghouse, who gained fame and fortune as the inventor of the air brake for railcars, thereby making them much safer to operate. The interchange and public debate between Edison and Tesla / Westinghouse became known as "The Current War."

Thomas Alva Edison was arguably the most prolific American inventor of all-time. Throughout his lifetime, Edison held over 1,000 American patents on a myriad of inventions. In addition to his capability as an inventor, Edison was also an entrepreneur who brought many of his inventions to market through his primary company, Edison Electric, which later merged with the Thomson-Houston Electric Company to form General Electric in 1893. The "Wizard of Menlo Park" was born in 1847 in Milan, Ohio. As a youngster, he lived in a rural community and was primarily self-educated, lacking any formal college or university education. However, he harbored an inquisitive mind that sought creative solutions to problems of everyday life. He was trained in his later-teens in telegraphy, and in 1866, at age nineteen, he took a job with Western Union in Louisville, Kentucky as the operator of the Associated Press bureau telegraph line. His early experience with sending and receiving information sent electronically over a wire led to an intense interest in electricity and electronic devices. His first American patent, granted in 1869 when he was twenty-two, was for an electric vote recorder.

A young Thomas Edison in his early thirties.

Edison resigned from Western Union in 1869 and began devoting himself to a lifetime occupation as a professional inventor. From 1869 to 1876 he operated a machine shop and employed model builders to make prototypes of the many products of his fruitful mind. In 1876, he established an "invention factory" in Menlo Park, New Jersey. His laboratory was staffed by loyal assistants and became a place of withdrawal for Edison were he had a degree of seclusion, free from organizational bureaucracy. The mission for his subordinates at Menlo Park was a minor invention every 10 days and a "big thing" every six months. Some of his most notable inventions, such as the incandescent lamp (known as the Edison Lamp) and carbon-filament light bulb were products of his time at Menlo Park. Other inventions credited to Edison in his lifetime were DC electric power systems, motion pictures, the stock ticker, phonograph, and an electric iron ore separator.

Edison carefully cultivated his public image. He claimed a disdain for science, little need for sleep, and explained his invention methodology as hunt-and-try. His actions were all carefully crafted to surround himself with an air of invincible creative genius, mystery, and secrecy—all intended to keep himself in the public spotlight and to serve as a device for raising capital for his company. His public image, however, was particularly heightened by his DC power system in New York City. Edison began building his direct current electric power transmission system in 1881 on Pearl Street in New York City. His system depended upon generating stations every few miles because DC current could not be conducted over long distances due to resistance in the transmission wires. He believed DC was safe to handle and the future for a nationwide power transmission system. In reality, however, his generation system was expensive and its initial customers limited to the wealthy, such as J. P. Morgan and the Vanderbilt's, or theaters, which used his electricity for special effects lighting. Nevertheless, in both his and the public's mind, Edison was the premier American inventor and master of electricity; therefore, any system challenging his supposed limitless talents and ingenuity was bound to be excoriated by him.

Edison's primary competitor in the field of electricity and power transmission systems was Nikola Tesla, a Serbian-American. Born in 1858 in a part of Serbia that is now Croatia, Tesla was an inventor, electrical and mechanical engineer, physicist, and futurist. Tesla was handsome, thin, over six feet tall, dressed elegantly, and later moved with the social and financial elite, becoming the personification of the mysterious creative genius. Tesla is best known as the inventor of the modern alternating current power transmission system, but recently has gained renown as a predictor of the future. He believed, in the early twentieth century, that telephone communications, as well as automobiles and airplanes, would someday be conducted and controlled wirelessly from ground transmission stations. He grew up in a rural environment, but he was bright enough to attend the Austrian Polytechnic University in Graz, Austria. He left after two years over disagreements with his advisor on the future direction for power generation, but he later studied at the University of Prague. While receiving his university education, Tesla became a strong believer in the superiority of polyphase power transmission, or alternating current. He thought that AC was safer, cleaner, and could be transmitted over longer distances than DC, thereby becoming less expensive as a source around which to build a power transmission system. After his time in Prague, Tesla moved to Budapest and took a job with the Budapest Telephone Exchange as their chief electrician. Similar to Edison, both inventors had exposure to telegraphy and telephony early in their careers. Unlike Edison, however, Tesla was university-educated.

In 1882, Tesla left Budapest and took a job with Continental Edison in France. Thomas Edison heard about this bright young man and offered Tesla a position in his New York City laboratory. After immigrating to the United States in 1884, Tesla worked for two years at Edison Electric. One of his first assignments was redesigning Edison's array of DC generators and making them more efficient. During the course of his work, Tesla tried to convince Edison of the superiority of AC on several occasions, but he was spurned by the celebrated inventor. Simply put, Edison did not want to be told his power system was inferior to something suggested by a university-educated novice who worked for him. Tesla completed the work and anticipated a promised $50,000 bonus. Rather than a bonus, Tesla was given a raise of $10 a month for a total monthly salary of $28. He declined the offer and resigned in 1886.

Nikola Tesla at age 34.

Upon resigning from Edison Electric, Tesla formed several small companies in 1886 and 1887. He devoted himself to developing alternating current power generation equipment. Financially this was a difficult time for him as one company failed, and Tesla, a brilliant engineer, was forced to take a series of menial jobs to support himself. However, inventively, this was an extremely productive period in his life. In 1887 he designed and patented an induction motor for AC current by utilizing a rotating magnetic field. His other significant inventions were a transformer which converted high-voltage AC to safer DC for use in homes and factories, and an AC generator. These three patents were purchased by George Westinghouse in 1888 and became the basis for the AC power transmission system offered by Westinghouse Electric. The landscape of power generation now had two well-financed and competing approaches: DC and Edison and AC with the partnership of Tesla / Westinghouse.

The "Current War" officially began in the late 1880s and continued through much of the 1890s. Edison was adamant that AC current was unsafe and impractical for use in homes due to the danger of electrocution from the high-voltage. He downplayed the high-cost of DC systems due to their profligate use of copper wire and series of intermediate power stations. He banked upon his public renown to popularize DC systems. He was, however, a strong believer that AC was useful for executing criminals through electrocution. His company, Edison Electric, designed and patented an AC-powered electric chair in 1888. He initially tested his electric chair on animals, then convinced the New York State Bureau of Prisons to switch from hanging to electrocution in 1888. In 1890 in New York, the first two criminals were electrocuted using Edison's chair. The use of electricity, seen by the public as a force for progress, to execute criminals revolted many potential customers. The electric chair caper tarnished Edison's reputation and was seen by many as an instrument by which he promoted his DC system.

The first electric chair designed by Edison Electric. The picture is from *Scientific American*, June 30, 1888.

The 1893 World's Fair in Chicago, also known as the Columbian Exposition, was a key battle between DC and AC. General Electric had placed a bid to power the jubilee using a DC system. Westinghouse did not submit a bid, but another Chicago contractor did submit one for an AC system using Westinghouse components. Westinghouse quickly agreed to supply the components, and the resulting bid was much lower than the competing GE bid, so the Columbian Exposition was powered using an AC system. Prior to and throughout the Fair, Westinghouse had to design many AC components in such a manner that they did not infringe upon GE patents. A last-minute lawsuit by GE alleging patent infringement by Westinghouse was dismissed, and the Fair, after much tribulation, was AC powered.

The DC and AC systems were also demonstrated at the Exposition. Edison designed an 80 foot tower, using 10,000 electric lamps, and 10,000 cut-glass panes to create a stunning display of the power of DC systems for the public. Tesla was known for his dramatic demonstration of the properties of high-voltage AC generated electricity. He built several AC powered exhibits to include his induction motors and AC powered generators. He also demonstrated several effects of the properties of AC power, such as a wireless gas-discharge lamp. The battle between the competing electric power transmission systems was on display for an eager public.

The final battles in the "Current War" entailed awarding contracts for long distance transmission. In 1890, the DC generating system at the Willamette Falls Station in Oregon City, Oregon was destroyed by a flood. It was replaced later that year with an AC system built by Westinghouse. While Willamette was the first AC system for long-distance transmission, the area was relatively sparsely populated. Much more fanfare, and competition, revolved around the selection of a current for the Niagara Falls Station in New York. As a well-known landmark and a utility near the heart of the population center for the United States, whichever current was selected would be a model for other generation systems throughout the country. In 1893 the Niagara Falls Power Company selected AC, because it could be generated and transmitted cheaper than DC, as the current of choice. Westinghouse won the contract for generating AC power and split the transmission line and transformer contracts with GE.

By 1893, General Electric and Westinghouse formed a duopoly

and controlled virtually the entire market for electrical generation equipment, transformers, meters, motors, and household lighting. One company promoted DC, the other AC. However, the decision to use AC current for the Niagara Falls hydroelectric project was a strong signal that future power generation projects undertaken by utility companies would prefer AC. Alternating current became the standard current used for such projects, and it was converted for household use through a transformer that made it safe for users. In time, General Electric developed a line of AC products to compete with Westinghouse, but they played a lagging role for many years.

The great advantage of AC current was that it could be transmitted more cheaply than DC current over great distances. Power could be generated in one location and sent over wires to another, with little loss due to resistance. For industrialists, factories were no longer constrained to being co-located with their power source, and they could be built virtually anywhere desired to better service their customers. For households, the plethora of AC transformers and motors made the high-voltage electricity safe to use, at least as safe as DC. The convenience of AC systems, along with their cost, were the great benefits over DC systems.

Edison's belief in his own creative genius, preference for direct current, and his public persona blinded him to the many benefits of AC current. He was supremely confident of his approach because he was recognized as the paramount electrical inventor of the late nineteenth century. He did not envision a potentially competing system for power generation to his and his company's financial detriment. Technological creativity within the field of AC, emanating from Nikola Tesla, eventually allowed it to be safely and cheaply transmitted long distances, something DC could not offer. If Edison had any misgivings about his unyielding support for DC, he did not state them publicly. He merely belatedly championed the development of AC systems at General Electric, which, while not an admission he was wrong, was a signal than AC was the current of the future for power generation.

Edison could not see the potential utility of AC current because he was overconfident in his DC system and a prisoner of his past experience.

Edison carefully cultivated his public image and in doing so began to believe his accolades as an inventive genius unparalleled by anyone else. Edison believed that he could succeed where others had failed, and this included designing a nationwide power transmission system. His hubris and shortsightedness prevented him from contemplating that components for an AC system—generators, transformers, and motors—could be designed and built making the high-voltage current safe to use in cities, factories, homes, and in rural America. While arguably the greatest American inventor of the late nineteenth and early twentieth centuries, Thomas Edison was wrong about the future for electrical transmission systems in America and the rest of the world.

CHAPTER FOUR

Contrary Views

*If we are all in agreement on the decision—then
I propose we postpone further discussion of this
matter until our next meeting to give ourselves time
to develop disagreement and perhaps gain some
understanding of what the decision is all about.*

–Alfred P. Sloan, former Chairman
and CEO of General Motors

The Concept

By now in this handbook a very consistent theme is emerging for building decision making skills. More options and diversity of thought clearly lead to better decisions. To achieve these two conditions Perceptive Leaders understand the need to explicitly search for **Contrary Views** (not just diversity of thought) from people who hold strongly opposing viewpoints. Alfred Sloan, renowned President and CEO of General Motors for 34 years, was famous for seeking the opposite opinion.

The confirmation bias is well known and extensively studied. For example, in a meta-analysis of 91 research studies, social psychologist William Hart and a group of fellow researchers discovered that humans are twice as likely to believe confirming evidence as disconfirming evidence. This bias manifests itself in organizations when we choose teams or hire people. We are drawn to individuals who are thoughtful and intelligent—people, coincidentally, just like ourselves!

A discussion on the confirmation bias would be incomplete without mentioning the concept of groupthink. The term groupthink was coined by research psychologist Irving Janis, who defines groupthink as "a powerful source of defective judgment that arises in cohesive groups—the concurrence-seeking tendency, which fosters over optimism, lack of vigilance, and sloganistic thinking about the weakness and immorality of out-groups." Often members of cohesive groups, even when holding a contrary opinion from the majority, do not feel comfortable sharing that view for fear of being an outsider.

Two techniques are well documented in seeking and obtaining opposing viewpoints. The first technique is to explicitly assign a person to collect disconfirming evidence against an alternative being considered. Sometimes called assigning a *devil's advocate*, this designation raises the probability that an opposing view is considered and also encourages team members to have the courage to challenge the prevailing opinion in a productive and safe manner. Edward de Bono developed a similar but more complex method that he calls the *Six Thinking Hats*, where team members are assigned different colored hats to ensure diversity of thought. In de Bono's process, the black hat is reserved for the explicit contrary views.

The second technique is quite effective when not only evaluating a decision alternative but also in the strategic execution planning process, and was developed by research psychologist Gary Klein. Most people are familiar with a post-mortem exercise, where clinicians gather, after a patient has died, to evaluate the cause of death. Klein's technique, called a "pre-mortem" exercise, requires the team to assume the decision was made and implemented, with negative outcomes … in other words, the patient died. Team members then discuss why the "patient died" or the decision failed. This discussion allows contrary views to emerge.

Perceptive Leaders recognize that proactively seeking contrary views requires explicit actions, not just a desire to "be objective" in seeking options. These two techniques can encourage serious consideration of significantly different alternatives, thereby ensuring better final outcomes.

What Should I Do as a PERCEPTIVE Leader to Encourage Contrary Views?

- Put people on your team who you know have opposing views to yours, not just diverse opinions generally.

- Assign someone or a group of people to seek disconfirming evidence—to play the devil's advocate.

- Allow every member of the team to play the contrary role for development opportunities, just as debaters must be prepared to argue either side of an issue.

- Before a final decision is made, conduct a pre-mortem exercise. Pretend the "patient died" and discuss why.

Case Study

President John Fitzgerald Kennedy, the Cold War, and the Cuban Missile Crisis

Key Points

- The case of the Cuban Missile Crisis (as well as earlier international decisions by President Kennedy) includes lessons on the importance of obtaining relevant information, using information most effectively, and ensuring that a devil's advocate is used when evaluating a potential decision.

- In making the decision to invade Cuba at the Bay of Pigs, President Kennedy relied on only a few sources of information without looking for opposing views. The invasion was unsuccessful, and this decision has become a classic case of groupthink.

- Partially because of the failed decision at the Bay of Pigs, President Kennedy was hesitant to make any moves to stop Russia from dividing Berlin. As he awaited "perfect" information, Russia began the construction of the Berlin Wall, and Kennedy was too late to act.

- Finally, during the Cuban Missile Crisis, President Kennedy was able to obtain reliable, relevant, and objective information. He also had improved his decision making process by evaluating an option using his diverse cabinet and military advisors and by explicitly seeking contrary views.

- Leaders need to make decisions without complete information, so it is critical that they ensure they obtain objective and relevant information when possible, and test any decision with contrary views.

The Story

John Fitzgerald Kennedy was the youngest person ever elected to the office of President of the United States. President Kennedy took office on January 20, 1961 at the height of the Cold War, a tense and precipitous time for a young leader. His primary adversary, at least internationally, was Nikita Khrushchev, the Premier of the Soviet Union. Khrushchev intended to test the resolve of the new American leader, a person whom he initially believed, was weak and possessed neither the skills nor resolve to confront the Soviet Union. Kennedy faced several crises within the first few months of his inauguration.

President Kennedy's first international crisis was the Bay of Pigs Invasion of Cuba in April 1961. Kennedy was an ardent anti-communist, and in his campaign for the presidency against Richard Nixon, the then candidate made several insinuations that the United States needed to invade Cuba to insure the downfall of Fidel Castro's regime. Kennedy desired to regain the momentum in the Cold War. There was great alarm in the United States over the fall of Cuba to a Marxist-Leninist force only 90 miles from the Florida Keys. This fact made the future of Cuba an extremely broiling domestic political issue. Coupled with the Soviet launch of the first manned orbital flight around Earth earlier in the year, Kennedy felt compelled to act. Almost from the day he assumed office, Kennedy was reviewing invasion plans with his top political advisor, Walt Rostow, and Director of the Central Intelligence Agency, Allen Dulles. Most of the information available to the CIA came from Cuban exiles living in the United States, or informers still residing in Cuba. In either case, basing a decision upon information gleaned from sources with a vested interest in the outcome—the downfall of Castro—portended perilous implications. Additionally, JFK did not seek contrary or opposing views, and his principal advisors did not challenge him. His Bay of Pigs decision was a classic case of "groupthink."

The vanguard of the invasion was to be Brigade 2506, a paramilitary unit of 1,400 Cuban exiles. This force was trained by the CIA in Guatemala. Code named Operation Zapata, the ground force was to conduct an amphibious landing on the southern coast of Cuba, conduct a link-up operation with anti-Castro forces living in Cuba, defeat Castro's revolutionary army, and eventually overthrow Castro. Also assisting the invasion were several CIA-trained Cuban exiles piloting American aircraft, under the supervision of American airmen. The air forces were to destroy Cuban air assets and airstrips to prevent reinforcement of any Cuban forces sent to reinforce the landing beaches. There were twenty U. S. Navy ships and submarines supporting the operation. Dulles and the CIA all agreed the plan was destined to work, an example of groupthink. There were few dissenting opinions that the operation would be anything but successful since the CIA had previously overthrown regimes in Nicaragua and Guatemala. Cuba was thought to be similar to these previous operations.

The invasion began on April 17th and was a catastrophe from the start. Cuba and the Soviet Union both knew the date and time of the planned invasion, on account of double-agents in the employ of both Castro and the CIA. After a few initial gains, Cuban revolutionary forces quickly recovered and surrounded Brigade 2506 on the beaches of the Bay of Pigs. There was little promised overt American support of the CIA operation from the U. S. Navy. Finally, there was almost no local support in Cuba for the invasion. Any local who may have supported the CIA-trained invaders had previously been rounded-up and imprisoned by Castro. Clearly, the CIA had overestimated anti-Castro sentiment on the island. By April 20th, merely three days after the invasion, 176 soldiers of Brigade 2506 had been killed and over 1,200 captured. Some of the prisoners were executed, but almost 1,100 were repatriated to the United States in 1962 in exchange for $53 million in food and medical supplies.

The Bay of Pigs Invasion was an unmitigated disaster and humiliation for President Kennedy. He had authorized an invasion with very little available information other than erroneous CIA estimates, confirmed by Cuban exiles living in Miami, declaring the weakness of

Castro's revolutionary army and the strength of anti-Castro sentiment in Cuba. The CIA intelligence failures were compounded by a cadre of advisors to Kennedy who saw a successful invasion as a predetermined outcome, based upon past experience. President Kennedy had fallen prey to subjective information. Ironically, an operation that intended to depose Castro, in fact strengthened his hand and virtually guaranteed that the Soviet Union would come to the assistance of their client state in the future.

President Kennedy's next major crisis was the construction of the Berlin Wall in August 1961. JFK was committed to stay in Berlin and not be driven out gradually or by force. Khrushchev believed West Berlin was an eyesore to be eliminated, and one of his favorite metaphors about the city was that it was a "bone stuck in the throat that must be disgorged." After the Bay of Pigs fiasco, Khrushchev felt that his opinion of Kennedy as a light-weight leader had been confirmed. The president of the German Democratic Republic (East Germany) was Walter Ulbricht, and he desired that West Berlin be isolated. In June 1961, Ulbricht made a speech in which he mentioned closing access to West Germany from East Germany. The result was a stream of refugees flooding from east to west. In early August 1961, Ulbricht proposed to Khrushchev that all East German borders be closed, including Berlin. Khrushchev agreed, and on August 13th a barbed wire barrier was strung around West Berlin, then eventually a wall around the periphery of the city. President Kennedy had no information available to counter the East German and Soviet action, but he remained committed to supporting access to West Berlin. JFK did not know construction of a wall was imminent and backed down because he had no information and did not want to escalate the situation. The construction of the Berlin Wall had unintended consequences for East Germany and the Soviet Union. The action was seen as brutal, the wall a moral obscenity, and virtually guaranteed that reunification of the city, not to mention Germany, would never occur under East German or Soviet auspices.

The Cuban Missile Crisis was the closest the world has ever come to nuclear war. The standard reading of this Cold War clash between the United States and the Soviet Union is that Khrushchev had contempt for President Kennedy and desired to exploit his supposed weakness as a leader, as demonstrated by the Bay of Pigs Invasion and construction of the Berlin Wall. Recent evidence demonstrates that Khrushchev actually saw Kennedy as aggressive and not passive, and believed that the West was winning the Cold War. Western democracies and economies were flourishing, while Marxism-Leninism was delivering less than promised. He sought to save Cuba and its revolution and bolster the image of the Soviet Union worldwide.

The deployment of nuclear missiles to Cuba was a joint decision reached by Castro and Khrushchev and was a response to American provocations to eliminate Castro. Both these leaders believed President Kennedy was going to authorize another invasion. The presence of a nuclear force so close to the United States was believed to be a deterrent for any future invasion of the island. In addition to protecting Castro and Cuba, Khrushchev saw the deployment of missiles as a response to the American placement of Jupiter nuclear missiles in Turkey in early 1962.

The secret deployment of the Soviet missiles was done in September and early October 1962. It was a major logistical undertaking and hugely successful. The Soviets deployed medium and intermediate range nuclear missiles, bombers, fighters, anti-aircraft assets, and tens of thousands of troops. A total of 42 nuclear missiles were capable of hitting nearly any target in the continental Unites States. The element of secrecy was crucial to achieving the Cuban—Soviet intended strategy; therefore, avoiding American inquiries required lying at the highest reaches of government. However, once discovered, the secrecy of the operation combined with the intense pressure placed upon President Kennedy concerning Cuba from the Congress, the press, and public opinion almost guaranteed some sort of strong American response, something Khrushchev did not anticipate.

During this crisis, President Kennedy was the beneficiary of very clear and vivid information. Unlike previous crises, such as the Bay of Pigs Invasion, the information available to him was recently and repeatedly obtained, and was of the highest quality. American U-2 reconnaissance overflights of Cuba had seen a Soviet military build-up, but not until October 15th were photographic images of missiles seen. This data was confirmed on October 16th. The President did not initially reveal this intelligence to the Soviets or American public. He met with Soviet Foreign Minister Andrei Gromyko on October 18th about the Soviet military build-up, and Gromyko denied the presence of any nuclear missiles.

Over the course of the next four days, President Kennedy met with his Executive Committee to discuss a response. Evidence demonstrates that his principal advisor was his brother Robert, then the Attorney General. Robert McNamara, the Secretary of Defense, and the chiefs of the service branches were on the ExComm, but they were primarily used as a group from which the President built consensus on courses of actions previously divined by him and his brother. Many options were examined to include a blockade of Cuba, interception of Cuban-bound shipping, another invasion of the island, placing American nuclear forces on alert, conducting probes of Soviet airspace, and preparations for a military response, nuclear options included, directed at the Soviet Union itself.

The military chiefs advocated a strong armed response—another invasion of Cuba or even portions of the Soviet Union—something the president and his brother wished to avoid. In this crisis, the military chiefs offered views contrary to what JFK and RFK had developed, and unintentionally played the role or devil's advocate for the president. JFK guarded against "groupthink" by arriving at a predetermined decision and then presenting it for debate to his hawkish military advisors.

President Kennedy revealed the presence of nuclear weapons in Cuba on October 22nd in a nationally televised address. The Soviet action shocked Americans, as well as the rest of the world. The world teetered on the brink of nuclear war. Kennedy mistakenly believed, based upon intelligence estimates, that there was parity between the nuclear forces of the United States and the Soviet Union, when in fact the number of American nuclear warheads outnumbered the Soviet Union by a ratio of 17:1. Over the next few weeks intense negotiations took place, often through secret channels, between the United States and the Soviet Union until a compromise solution was reached. The nuclear missiles, as well as Soviet troops on the island were withdrawn. In return, the United States agreed to remove the Jupiter missiles from Turkey and promised they would not invade Cuba in the future. Castro would remain in power and Cuba continue as a Communist state for the balance of the Cold War. After the Cuban Missile Crisis, the Cold War became a bit more stable and predictable, even though it lasted for another 27 years.

Popular accounts have described the Cuban Missile Crisis as a model for decision making in a strategic emergency, as well as an American "victory" in the Cold War. President Kennedy, rightfully, was lauded for his leadership. However, the final outcome was clearly a compromise in which both sides relented in some of their demands, in return for averting nuclear war. The final resolution of the crisis was the result, in part, of reliable, recently obtained, repeatedly collected, and vivid information being available to American decision makers. There was no denying the presence of missiles once the photographic evidence was obtained by the U-2 reconnaissance flights. In the absence of such high-quality information, the aftermath may have been much different.

There are several observations on the relationship between President Kennedy's available information and the outcomes from the crises he faced. First, the information that he obtained became progressively more reliable, therefore it led to better decisions and outcomes. During the Bay of Pigs invasion, the only available information came from Cuban exiles who were hostile to Castro and his regime. Subjective information of this caliber is often unreliable. There was virtually no available information prior to East German construction of the Berlin Wall; therefore, American courses of action were severely limited. Conversely, hard objective data, such as photographs, from the U-2 reconnaissance flights over Cuba, allowed the Kennedy Administration space and time to negotiate an amicable end to the crisis. There is a difference between objective information and subjective information. While both can, and should be used, during the decision making process, more weight is normally assigned to objective information.

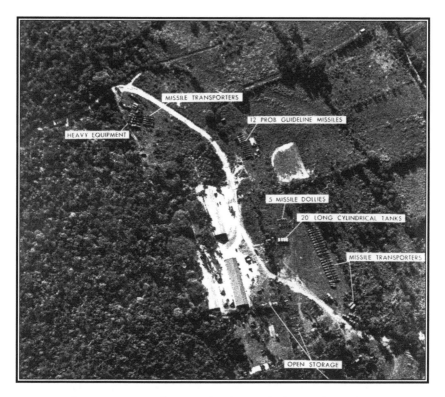

Reconnaissance photograph taken early during the Cuban
Missile Crisis showing medium-range missiles.

Second, by the time of the Cuban Missile Crisis, President Kennedy
had changed and streamlined his decision making process. He sought
contrary views, unlike in the Bay of Pigs and Berlin Wall crises.
Additionally, he arrived at a decision prior to meeting with ExComm
and used this body, primarily the military chiefs, as devil's advocates.
This approach allowed for a wide ranging discussion of options, yet
maintained primary focus on actions short of a full-scale military
response and potential nuclear engagement with the Soviets.

Third, the quality of information during the Cuban Missile Crisis
was extremely vibrant. It fit all the criteria leaders need for information;
it was recently obtained, repeatedly confirmed through additional
surveillance flights, and was vivid and of the highest quality. In this
instance, the President had adequate information to make an informed
and intelligent response.

Finally, during the Cuban Missile Crisis in particular, there was no time to collect endless reams of data. Nevertheless, the available information established the presence of nuclear missiles, and this was the crucial information required for an American response. The lesson is that very often leaders must act with incomplete information, but they need to ensure the information they can obtain is as objective, and as relevant to the decision, as possible. And before making a final decision, they need to take some time to "test" the decision with contrary views before acting.

CHAPTER FIVE

External Landscape

*Even as the Federal Reserve continues prudent
planning for the ultimate withdrawal of monetary
policy accommodation, we also recognize that the
economic outlook remains unusually uncertain.*

–Ben Bernanke, Federal Reserve
Chairman on July 21, 2010

The Concept

In the introduction, we argued that leaders can raise the probability of a good outcome in two ways—they can build their skills and they can manage uncertainty more effectively. A foundational skill in managing uncertainty for a Perceptive Leader is the ability to evaluate the **External Landscape,** not just in the context of future trends, but also in the more nuanced perspective of known knowns, or certainties, and known unknowns, or uncertainties. How do they manage the uncertainties effectively, especially when the future outlook is "unusually uncertain"? The final six chapters focus on the capabilities and conditions to create a more Perceptive Organization that manages uncertainties.

In a news briefing for the US Department of Defense on February 12, 2002, Secretary of Defense Donald Rumsfeld famously said, "There are known knowns; there are things we know we know. There are known unknowns. That is to say there are things that we now know we don't know. But there are also unknown unknowns. There are things we do not know we don't know." A Perceptive Leader recognizes the truth in this statement: understanding the known knowns and known unknowns is the most effective way to continuously assess the external landscape.

Strategic planning groups spend an inordinate amount of time poring over research and data to study future trends in their industries or professions. The Perceptive Leader takes a more distinctive view around future forces, devoting resources to distinguishing between future known knowns, or future certainties, and future known unknowns, or future uncertainties. In fact, the way in which senior leaders strategically address the certainties should differ dramatically from the way the uncertainties are addressed. Specifically, strategic planning groups should *plan* for certainties and *manage* uncertainties. This capability is particularly important in the current VUCA environment.

We begin with an examination of strategic *certainties*. Using the delivery of health care in the United States as an example, many uncertainties exist for the future: the exact cost of health care, new ways in which technology will be used in delivering the care, the types of diseases that will be cured or will emerge, and the reimbursement model for health systems. But there is one (almost 100%) certainty for the future in the delivery of health care: more care delivery will shift from inpatient care in acute care hospitals to outpatient care in ambulatory settings or in the home. Why? Technology is allowing this to happen, the cost is less overall, and outpatient care is literally safer than inpatient care, where infections can thrive.

Even though this phenomenon is a known known, or certainty, hospitals and health systems (at least in the United States) do not view this shift to outpatient care as financially positive for their hospitals, simply because bed occupancy is a revenue stream. A Perceptive health care system CEO understands that even though this certainty may have a negative impact on the health system, the health system would be remiss if it were not addressing and planning for that shift in its five-year strategic plan. Perceptive Leaders *strategically plan* for known knowns.

Let's consider strategic *uncertainties*. In Chapter Three on Range of Alternatives, we introduced the concept of decision rights—the practice of stating explicitly who will make the final decision and when the decision will be made. Often, even if a decision date is formalized, leaders will balk when the date arrives and push back, imploring, "But we can't make the decision—we still don't have all of the information. We still have uncertainties!" A decision maker may be able to eliminate some uncertainties with more information, but there are always uncertainties that cannot be eliminated. Consider the concept of *managing uncertainties* in the lean process, a key quality management tool developed initially in Japan by manufacturers such as Toyota. The ultimate goal of the lean process is to eliminate all variability in a process. However, engineers know that all variability cannot be eliminated, so they talk about *managing the variability*. The same phenomenon occurs in the strategic context with external uncertainties. Yes, leaders should eliminate uncertainties where they can; however, they also should recognize the need to manage those uncertainties they cannot control or influence.

Perceptive Leaders recognize they cannot wait to make a decision until there are no more uncertainties—this is simply not possible. Instead, they should make a decision and at the same time identify the key strategic uncertainties associated with that decision. This allows the Leader to anticipate potential areas of adaptability later in implementation. The Point du Hoc case in Chapter One on Purpose demonstrates that commanders must make a decision to move forward and then be prepared to adapt.

Another set of professionals facing both *certainties* and *uncertainties* are financial advisors and wealth managers. This profession now recognizes that in the future, robo-advisors (internet-based financial advising tools) will be used more frequently. For example, we have two children firmly in the millennial generation, born in 1990 and 1992. In the last year they have started to invest for their futures, as they are now earning more. They both used some traditional financial instruments such as mutual funds, but they also opened accounts with the app robinhood.com—accounts that they can manage from their phones. Robinhood.com has no minimum balance and no fees for transactions, and they can purchase partial shares of their favorite stocks. Our children are not in need of sophisticated financial advice at this stage in their careers. The use of these fintech tools is clearly a future known known, and any financial services company should be planning for this certainty. However, will the need for human financial advisors be completely eliminated in ten or twenty years? In the future when our children (hopefully) have accumulated some wealth, will they opt for human interaction or rely on their past experience with fintechs? A Perceptive Leader has no problem stating, "I don't know, and I am willing to say, "I don't know!"

Remembering the overconfidence bias from Chapter Three, the ability to say, "I don't know" does not come naturally, but it is a very important skill for senior leaders to develop. In the words of Nassim Nicholas Taleb, essayist and scholar, in his book, *Fooled by Randomness*, "We should start every meeting convincing everyone that we are a bunch of idiots who know nothing … but we happen to be endowed with the rare privilege of knowing it." Taleb is asserting that knowing what you don't know is a strategic strength.

One final nod to Donald Rumsfeld will close an important loop in this discussion. Rumsfeld also spoke of unknown unknowns. Taleb calls these forces *black swans*—forces that are very rare and highly unpredictable. Our view of unknown unknowns? Leaders can keep themselves awake at night imagining all sorts of scary scenarios but by definition, they still cannot truly anticipate them. However, executives who have honed their Perceptive Leadership skills may be able to see these unknown unknowns, figuratively, a split second before others, creating a competitive advantage.

When we were first married, we lived in Monterey, California and we were living in that idyllic area during the 1989 Loma Prieta earthquake. Those who have experienced an earthquake know there are aftershocks for days afterwards. At the time, we owned a large yellow Labrador retriever named Ben. Again, those readers who have experienced an earthquake and own a dog can guess our next point. Literally five to ten seconds before an aftershock, Ben's head would pop up and he would whine. He somehow could sense the movement before we could feel it. The overriding point? Perceptive Leaders can react like Ben and potentially see those unknown unknowns early. The importance of Vigilance is explored in a later chapter.

In summary, Perceptive Leaders understand the need to evaluate the external landscape by identifying both known knowns and known unknowns. They know that they need to *strategically plan* for known changes, and be willing to anticipate the need for adaptability with the uncertainties, or known knowns.

What Should I Do as a Perceptive Leader to Better Understand the External Landscape?

- Identify key certainties or known knowns over the next five years and then ensure you are planning for those certainties in your strategic planning process.

- Explicitly identify the uncertainties or known unknowns, particularly when making the final decision. Use these uncertainties to anticipate potential areas of adaptability in implementation.

- Be willing to say, as a leader, "I KNOW I don't know what is going to happen in the future."

Case Study

General George Washington and the Sieges of Boston and Yorktown

Key Points

- In the Siege of Boston, General Washington faced some certainties, or known knowns: the British army was larger and better-trained, the British navy was the best in the world, and his army would abandon their posts if they were static. General Washington planned for these certainties.

- General Washington also faced one key known unknown—the strategy of the British army in the battle around Boston. He and his advisors were somewhat paralyzed by this uncertainty, and the British forces gained the upper hand.

- After the Siege of Boston, Washington learned he needed to be proactive, even in the midst of uncertainty. Indecision with little movement was harmful in the Siege of Boston.

- He had also learned to be more adaptive since a leader can never eliminate the unknowns completely. Specifically, he appointed General Nathaniel Greene to lead American forces in the southern theatre. Greene knew how to leverage the Continental army's known strengths and weaknesses to exploit General Cornwallis of the British army, who had a strong experiential frame about traditional warfare. Greene's leadership in the southern theatre was essential in the eventual British defeat.

- In the Siege of Yorktown, Washington was able to learn more about his unknowns and converted them to knowns.

The Story

An organization may have a robust process for arriving at potential solutions to issues during their decision making process, but information about the competitive environment is never complete and always fraught with some degree of uncertainty. There is always information about the external environment and your opponent's strengths and weaknesses that is certain, and in nearly all cases, information that is unknown. When both known and unknown external information is combined with your assessment of an opponent's strengths and weaknesses, you can begin to discern the most likely course of action of your competition and formulate an effective strategy for your organization.

Obviously, the more known information is available, the better a quality decision. However, rarely will you know everything you desire before making a decision. An inordinate amount of time may be spent attempting to hedge your risk and "know everything." The time spent on collecting information, which may not measurably improve the quality of decision, may eventually limit the range of options you select.

General George Washington and Command of the Continental Army

The origins of the United States Army can be traced to armed hostilities beginning in 1775. The British commander in the Colonies was General Thomas Gage, and the majority of his force was stationed in and around Boston. In April 1775, Gage sent a British force to capture American gunpowder stores in Lexington and Concord, Massachusetts. After an unsuccessful operation, the British column of 1,500 soldiers began the trek back to Boston. Colonial militia units had been alerted and lined the route back to the British lines, inflicting 20 percent casualties on the Redcoats. In May 1775, American militia units under the command of Ethan Allen and Benedict Arnold captured the British garrisons at Fort Ticonderoga and Crown Point along the Lake Champlain corridor. Finally, British forces attacked and eventually dislodged an American force entrenched on Breed's Hill in Boston (mistakenly referred to as Bunker Hill), but at a terrible price, suffering almost 1,000 casualties out of their attacking force of 2,500 soldiers.

In June 1775, the Second Continental Congress, seated in Philadelphia, passed legislation creating the Continental Army. The man selected to command the Continental Army, and the militia units around Boston, was George Washington. He was regarded as one of the ablest American military commanders of the time due to his experience in the Seven Years War, also known as the French and Indian War. In this earlier war, he was given command of the Virginia Regiment, regarded as the most capable colonial unit of the war supporting British regular troops. Additionally, Washington was a Southerner, and his selection as commander of the Continental Army was designed to provide the rebellion a broader base of support and extend it to the southern colonies.

General George Washington before the Battle of Trenton. Painting by John Trumbull.

The Siege of Boston

The Siege of Boston began in April 1775. Washington tightened his grip on Boston for the balance of 1775 with the able assistance of his Chief of Artillery and former bookseller Henry Knox, and British ex-patriot Charles Lee who supervised construction of the trenches surrounding Boston. However, General Washington was faced with several knowns and unknowns at this point. First, he recognized that British land forces outnumbered his Continental Army and they were a much better trained, equipped, and disciplined fighting force. Additionally, America had no navy to speak of, and the British were the preeminent world naval power. Second, the Americans had little artillery surrounding Boston in 1775, so Washington recognized he must somehow get additional cannon into his siege lines to make a viable defensive perimeter around the British. Third, the longer his militia remained in static positions surrounding Boston, the greater the pull was for these men to leave the lines and return home to their full-time occupations. Somehow, Washington needed to break the stalemate. Finally, he had no idea what strategy the British would employ to break the static military situation around Boston, nor what path they would choose in their effort to defeat the young insurgency nationwide.

Washington's first action to break the stalemate, to keep his forces engaged in the rebellion, and to minimize British military strength was to invade Canada. Late in 1775, with the agreement of the Continental Congress, he launched an invasion of Canada with the intent of making it the fourteenth colony. The plan was to target the formerly French portions of Canada recently incorporated into British Canada. The assault was aimed at Montreal and Quebec City. While the assault on Montreal was successful, the attack on Quebec, under the command of Benedict Arnold and Daniel Morgan, failed miserably.

Washington's next action was to improve his firepower around Boston, particularly his artillery. He instructed Knox to move the artillery captured at Fort Ticonderoga to Dorchester Heights, south of Boston. From this commanding position, Washington reasoned that the British would be trapped inside Boston. Using sleds, during the winter of

1775—1776, Knox moved over 50 cannon. His forces were now stronger, but Washington also knew that he could not contain the British for an indefinite period of time, given their land and naval superiority.

Washington's final contemplated action during the Siege of Boston was a direct assault against the British. He envisioned an assault upon Boston from "The Neck" or southern side of the city. He convened a Council of War to discuss the proposal. In eighteenth- and nineteenth-century warfare, it was common for American commanders to use a Council of War prior to making important tactical or operational decisions. The Council was nearly always composed of the overall supreme commander, his subordinate unit commanders, and whatever staff officers the supreme commander believed could improve the decision to be made. General George Washington was the first American military officer to use a Council of War in the field.

His subordinate commanders talked Washington out of attacking Boston. They stressed the military difficulty of confronting a superior British force through a narrow peninsula. More importantly, they believed a pre-assault bombardment would destroy patriot property, cause civilian casualties, and generate strong resistance against the American rebellion. Washington reluctantly heeded their fears and canceled the assault. By the spring of 1776, the American and British forces around Boston were in a continued stalemate. While General Washington had attempted to address external knowns and unknowns and was successful to a degree, he ultimately never determined future British plans—his most vexing unknown. He awoke on a cold and misty morning March 17, 1776 and was surprised to find the city and harbor vacated by the British. By evacuating, the British sought to change the stalemated situation and direct a concerted effort at pacifying the rebellious colonies. Unintentionally, through inaction, Washington had surrendered the initiative to the British.

Washington and Developments Before the Siege of Yorktown

After the British vacated Boston, they moved their force initially to Halifax, Nova Scotia, then landed on Long Island. In the summer of

1776, Washington fought a series of losing engagements against the British in and around New York City and was chased through New Jersey. After conducting surprise raids against the British garrisons in Trenton and Princeton in December, Washington and his Army spent the winter encamped around Morristown, New Jersey. He had nearly lost his Army in New York City, but the experience was a major revelation for him. Since the British were better trained and supplied than the Americans, he realized he must avoid losing the Continental Army in a direct encounter with them and instead husband his scarce resources.

In 1777, the British occupied the rebel capital of Philadelphia. Encouraged by the Continental Congress to do something, Washington attempted to stop the British at the Brandywine River south of Philadelphia but suffered a humiliating defeat. In the fall, Washington attempted another surprise attack on Philadelphia and met the British at Germantown, Pennsylvania. Even with the element of surprise, the Americans could not hold their gains and retreated to Valley Forge to establish winter quarters. While Valley Forge is most remembered for the sacrifice and privation suffered by the Continental Army from the lack of supplies and nearly complete breakdown of their logistics apparatus, it was here that the Continental Army received drill, discipline, and training from the Prussian volunteer officer Baron von Steuben. He was a master trainer, and during the winter of 1777-1778 he drilled the Continental Army into a heightened state of readiness, thereby addressing the known training gap between American and British forces.

The great test for the Continental Army came in the spring of 1778. The new British commander, General Henry Clinton, saw little value in the continued occupation of Philadelphia, and he wished to combine all his forces for operations elsewhere. As Clinton started north towards New York City, Washington and the Continental Army met him at Monmouth Courthouse in New Jersey. The battle was a draw, but the most important aspect of the battle was the improved movement, drill, and discipline of the Continental Army. Monmouth Courthouse demonstrated that the Americans could field an army capable of defeating the British. It inspired great confidence in Washington and his men.

After Monmouth Courthouse, Washington never again risked a

major portion of the Continental Army. He had learned his lesson in New York City—the Americans could win, but in order to do so he must preserve the backbone of colonial resistance, the Continental Army, and prolong the war until the British tired of fighting. Thus was born what many historians have called Washington's "Fabian Strategy." It is so named after Roman Emperor Fabius, who in the third century BC, avoided direct combat with the Carthaginians under Hannibal in southern Italy and eventually defeated the Carthaginians by outlasting them. From 1778 through 1781, Washington spread the Continental Army to cover strongpoints from central New Jersey, through the Hudson highlands in New York, intensively prepared defensive positions at West Point, and extended his defenses into Connecticut. The British occupied New York City and Newport, Rhode Island, but in 1778, the Americans controlled everything outside these two port cities.

General George Washington at the Siege of Yorktown

The decisive theatre of the American Revolution was in the South. It was here that the war was won. The British southern strategy can be traced to December 1778 when they sent an expedition of 3,500 to capture Savannah. They easily occupied this city and the rest of Georgia. They planned to use Savannah as a base for further operations in America and the Caribbean. In early 1780 the British landed south of Charleston and during the course of a one-month siege the town surrendered. The fall of the garrison of 5,400 troops in May 1780, under the command of Benjamin Lincoln, was a serious blow to American military strength. Lincoln did little to thwart the landside investment by the British, and his naval forces were negligible. His troops outnumbered the British, but his inactivity resulted in the most significant American military loss of the entire war. The number of troops surrendered were the largest number in one battle in American military history, until World War Two. Reacting to the fall of Charleston, Congress appointed Horatio Gates as the commander of the Continental Army in the South. Gates promptly marched his 1,400 Continentals and militia to Camden, South Carolina in August 1780 in what became a decisive British victory.

Following the battle, Gates asked to be relieved and was replaced by Nathaniel Greene.

Washington now had more knowns than unknowns in 1780—1781, than he did in 1775—1776 outside Boston. First, a definitive British strategy was now apparent. They had continued to occupy large coastal cities and the supposed political center of the country in Philadelphia, while seldom venturing inland. This strategy had yet to bring the British decisive victory as their land forces never exceeded 50,000, a number insufficient to pacify an area stretching from New England to Georgia. Second, Washington had devised a strategy of his own by then. It was one of erosion—by never letting the Continental Army engage in a decisive battle and prolonging the war, he believed war weariness would force the British to quit the conflict. In other words, he could win by not losing. Finally, Washington now had the financial and military assistance of the French. The French had landed a ground force in New England and had two fleets operating in American and Caribbean waters. In short, he had a plan and knew with some clarity what the British intentions were, and thus he was in a much stronger military position.

After the fall of Charleston and occupation of several interior towns, British General in Chief Henry Clinton turned over command in the south to Lord Charles Cornwallis, convinced that the plan to pacify the south was working. However, the harsh treatment and persecution of Scots-Irish colonists by the British regulars and the use of Loyalist militia units derailed the British plan. The confiscation of property and crops by the British inflamed the locals, and the Loyalists often exacted revenge for personal grievances, thereby adding further fuel to the conflagration. These actions changed the formerly neutral southern colonists into supporting the rebellion. Ultimately, when the British lost the support of the southern colonists, their campaign was doomed.

The appointment of Greene was a masterstroke. He understood that he was too weak to face the British in a traditional European-style battle, but if he could draw Cornwallis into the interior and use the new found support of partisans, guerillas, and militia units in the South, he could exhaust British combat power by forcing them to leave regular army units to pacify captured areas. Greene came to rely upon the support of partisan commanders in South Carolina. These men conducted ferocious guerilla warfare against British regulars and Loyalist militia in the Carolinas and Virginia. Their resistance was highlighted at the battles of Kings Mountain and Cowpens, South Carolina in October 1780 and January 1781, respectively.

Greene let Cornwallis chase him into Virginia, then doubled back to meet Cornwallis at Guilford Courthouse, North Carolina in March 1781. Greene had 4,500 Continentals and militia versus 2,000 for the British. The British casualties were so high that Cornwallis had to retreat to Wilmington, North Carolina to get more troops and supplies. After resupply, Cornwallis headed north into Virginia, which he considered the heart of the rebellion in the South. Meanwhile, Greene moved back in to the Carolinas and Georgia where he won several small battles and eliminated the strung-out British garrisons. By September 1781, Greene's forces had gained effective control of the south except for Wilmington, Savannah, and Charleston.

Cornwallis headed into Virginia with 7,000 troops, but failed to bring the Continental Army into decisive battle. He moved to Yorktown on the York River in August 1781 and awaited either resupply or evacuation to New York City. Meanwhile, Washington had previously sent 3,000 troops from the north into northern Virginia under the command of Lafayette. These troops harassed Cornwallis and pinned him against the banks of the York River.

Washington directed that the French Navy seal off the Chesapeake and this was done by the two French fleets operating in the area in early September 1781. One fleet from the Caribbean engaged the British relief fleet sailing to Yorktown and pulled it away from the mouth of the Chesapeake Bay. In the meantime, a French fleet stationed off Rhode Island slipped in behind the British and sealed off the immediate area around Yorktown. Once the French fleet chased away the British fleet, this French fleet blockaded the outer approach to Yorktown at the mouth of the Chesapeake Bay. With the French controlling the York River and mouth of the Chesapeake Bay, Cornwallis was facing imminent disaster.

Washington left a small force surrounding New York City and made a few feints—enough to fool Clinton into thinking he was planning a major assault against the city. This tactic was enough to make Clinton hesitate until it was too late to send a ground force to relieve Cornwallis. General Washington collected and moved 7,000 French troops under French General Rochambeau, 5,700 Continental Army, and 3,000 local militia and surrounded Cornwallis as he sat in Yorktown pondering his fate. The siege of Yorktown began in early September 1781 and concluded on October 19, 1781. The Americans and French bombarded the city and continued to creep their lines closer to the British, all the while eliminating potential escape routes. Once Cornwallis realized that he was neither being resupplied nor relieved, and that all his escape routes were closed, he surrendered.

The American victory at Yorktown, with significant French assistance, permanently shifted British public opinion against the war. General Washington had fully made use of external knowns to mitigate unknown information during the Siege of Yorktown to gain a stunning victory. He had won by not losing the Continental Army and prolonging the war for six long years.

Lessons Learned

There are several transferable lessons learned from General Washington's actions during the American Revolution. First, decision makers will never have complete information and at some point must delineate a course of action. At the outset of the conflict, he was faced with much more unknown than known information. While encamped around Boston, Washington was assessing his strengths and weaknesses and had determined his land and naval forces were inferior to the British, yet he had no overarching strategy or desired outcome at that time. He certainly had little idea what future courses of action the British contemplated. As a result, he launched the ill-fated expedition to Canada, and the British eventually slipped away from his grasp and headed to New York City. Washington then risked his army in very perilous actions around New York City. His decision making in the early years of the conflict was done in the context of little known external information. Decision makers will seldom have all information they desire, yet must act based upon what they know, and Washington's decision was almost fatal.

Second, Washington gained better information over time, by converting unknown to known information, thus resulting in more successful outcomes. He was able to adapt, and also eliminate some uncertainties over time. He noticed that the British occupied major coastal cities that were also the political centers of the nation—Boston, Newport, New York, Philadelphia, and Charleston. British actions also demonstrated that they were reluctant to venture too far inland in pursuit of the rebels and risk their military forces. Furthermore, using this approach, the British were never able to pacify the rural areas of the former colonies. After determining overall British strategy, Washington was able to develop a successful American strategy. As long as he did not lose the Continental Army and prolonged the conflict, the better the chance for eventual victory and independence. General Washington, always cognizant of his strengths and weaknesses in comparison to the British, converted more unknown external information to known information, thereby facilitating development of a successful strategy.

Finally, even with much more information available to him at Yorktown, Washington's plan at Yorktown was fraught with risk. Seldom are decision makers faced with "no-brainers" or riskless decisions. Leaders will always still have uncertainties, or risks, so they must manage the risk. Yorktown was a very complicated land and naval action for the late eighteenth century. Washington had neither direct communication nor command of the French fleets, which were critical to blocking British resupply or evacuation from Yorktown. He merely gave the French a general outline of his intended plan. Additionally, he risked losing the portion of the Continental Army left outside New York City to the British if they attacked while he took the majority of his forces south to Virginia. He made several calculated estimates of potential British responses to his actions based upon his experience during six years of war. Fortunately, he had more known information at Yorktown than unknown.

CHAPTER SIX

Productive Paranoia

*Productive paranoia isn't a negative attribute,
it's more of a strategy to ensure your business
stays in business for years to come.*

–Jim Collins, business management
consultant and author

The Concept

Chapter Two introduced the concept of experiential frames, a common critical thinking barrier. Just like humans, organizations also build a view of the world based on the organization's past. Anecdotal evidence indicates the older and more successful an organization, the stronger that view or set of assumptions that have developed over time based on these past experiences. Perceptive Leaders understand that organizations must be willing to demonstrate **Productive Paranoia** as a way to challenge these assumptions and thus be better prepared for an uncertain future.

According to Jim Collins in *Great by Choice*, where he introduces the term, organizations that manage uncertainty most effectively exhibit productive paranoia, or the willingness to challenge these long-held organizational beliefs. Some organizations refer to these assumptions as their *organizational mental model*. The goal for senior leaders is not to eliminate the organizational mental model, but rather acknowledge it, surface the assumptions within the mental model and be willing to challenge those assumptions on a frequent basis. We offer two concrete examples of organizational assumptions.

An automobile company with which Kathy worked had a major assumption, based on its very successful past, that the larger the population in an area, the more cars the company would sell in that area. In other words, the company had observed a strong positive correlation between population size and demand for automobiles. Thus, the company's demand forecasts historically were based on this assumption. This organization ignored any challenges to that assumption, to include two known knowns that have recently emerged. These two forces did, indeed, begin as uncertainties, but recent data confirms these are now truly known trends: the continued rise in urbanization and ride sharing. Many articles have been written about the millennial generation and now the emerging Generation Z delaying learning to drive and choosing *not* to buy an automobile. Also, urban areas are beginning to restrict the number of cars allowed within the city limits either explicitly, or by charging enormous parking fees and tolls to enter the city. These two forces have changed the relationship between population size and demand for cars, adversely affecting the organization's demand models in the future.

In another example, in March 2010 Kathy boarded a plane bound for Detroit after a long day of teaching. A woman sat next to her who shared she was a senior leader at Borders Group (owner of Borders Bookstores). She included others in conversation as she shared that Borders was struggling with the emerging trend of e-books and e-readers such as Amazon's Kindle and Barnes and Noble's Nook. (In fact, Apple would introduce the iPad the very next month.) She focused her discussion on ways Borders could entice customers back into the stores, not how Borders could adjust to customers' changing demands. As Kathy researched the history of Borders, she realized that its business model was partially dependent upon the customer experience in the store. This emphasis on building cool stores with music centers, coffee shops, and large comfortable couches became part of the Borders mental model of the pathway to continued success. Borders Bookstores profited from this world view, until the world changed around the organization. Borders filed for bankruptcy in 2013.

So, how do Perceptive Leaders both honor the history and experiences of their organizations but also seek to avoid the dangers of a strong mental model? First, they encourage the team to really analyze the organization, department, or business unit with an eye for deeply held beliefs. They recognize the importance of institutional knowledge and emphasize that challenging these widely held assumptions should not summarily dismiss the prior success of the organization. Finally, these leaders know that many assumptions may continue to be valid, but Perceptive Organizations have cultures that always promote broader thinking from their employees.

In conclusion, business pundits sometimes snicker at famous companies that eventually failed such Kodak, Blockbuster, and Blackberry, snidely commenting that "they just became too arrogant."

We offer the counter view that organizations that have been very successful have large historical data sets to explain that success. To quote Jim Collins, leaders who employ productive paranoia are not "avoiding danger, trying to find the safest and most enjoyable path through life" or "protecting what they have," but rather they are "creating and building something truly great, bigger than themselves." Perceptive Leaders learn to discern when the time is ripe for creating a new future.

What Should I Do as a Perceptive Leader to Promote Productive Paranoia?

- Encourage your teams and your staff to explicitly define the current organizational mental model. What are the key assumptions you utilize every day when making decisions about your environment, your workforce, your organizational capabilities, your customers, your competitors, and your business model?

- Challenge your employees to do this exercise not only for your organization at the macro level, but for their areas of responsibility. What does the manufacturing group assume, because that is how "it has always been?"

- Be explicit about areas of vulnerability if, in fact, those assumptions are wrong in the future. "What if people stop wanting automobiles at the same rate?"

Case Study

The American Shaving Market, Gillette, and the Rise of E-commerce

Key Points

- Gillette has had a long, successful history in the American shaving market.

- This history caused Gillette to build a strong organizational mental model that the organization was reluctant to challenge.

- Dollar Shave Club emerged as an e-commerce competitor that was inexpensive and irreverent.

- Gillette suffered a decrease in market share because of its inability to challenge the historical assumptions and only now has begun a shave club with less expensive options.

The Story

Throughout the nineteenth century, shaving was not a daily ritual for most men. The only device available for shaving facial hair at home was a straight-edge razor. The straight razor had to be periodically sharpened, most often at a barber shop, and honed on a leather strop before usage. Because these were time consuming processes, most men minimized their time allotted to shaving and exhibited some type of facial hair. In fact, all American presidents starting with Andrew Jackson (1828 to 1836) and running through the balance of the nineteenth century wore facial hair. Home shaving became more common in the early twentieth century thanks to King C. Gillette of Boston.

King C. Gillette, circa 1910.

Gillette was frustrated with having to bring his straight-edge razor to his local barber shop for sharpening, so in 1901 he founded the Gillette Company, originally known as the American Safety Razor Company. In 1904 Gillette received a patent on a "safety razor," which had a disposable, single-edge blade. The genius behind Gillette's razor was because steel fabrication and stamping techniques had progressed so rapidly in the late nineteenth century, such that he recognized that it had become economically feasible to mass-produce a single-edge blade. A customer simply unscrewed the top of the razor, threw away the old blade, inserted a new one, and when that blade became dull, he began the process again. Gillette also claimed that the shave was much closer than one from a straight-edge razor. Razor sales were brisk, reaching 91,000 units in 1904, with an additional 124 thousand replacement blades also sold. The "safety razor" retailed for $5 (over $150 in 2018 dollars), so Gillette improved upon its manufacturing techniques to lower the price. By 1915, Gillette was selling nearly half a million razors a year and in excess of 70 million replacement blades annually.

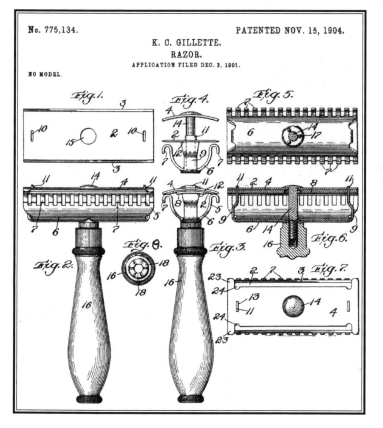

Gillette Safety Razor, 1904 Patent Application.

The Gillette Company grew tremendously throughout the twentieth century and dominated the American market for home shaving products. Their strategy was to lead through the application of scale to reduce unit costs, invest heavily in research and development, and constantly bring new products to market. Gillette claimed the new products produced ever-better shaves; therefore, they charged a premium price for them, and their advertising convinced customers to "trade-up" to the new product. The basic disposable single-blade was their primary product until the 1970s. However, in the 65 years since introducing the safety razor, the single blade became thinner, the edges were coated for smoother shaves, blade insertion into the razor was made easier, and razors were made adjustable for differing beard thicknesses in men. In 1971 Gillette introduced the Trac II, the first twin-blade razor; in 1998 the Mach III / Venus, a triple-blade razor; and in 2006 the Fusion series—a five-blade razor, complete with a pivoting head. The increasingly more sophisticated razors were also more expensive. The current top-of-the-line Gillette razor, the Fusion Proglide Flexball sells for $13, and a replacement package of four cartridges costs $20.

Gillette's strategy of providing a steady stream of new, premium-priced products and leveraging their well-known brand name proved to be very successful. By 2011, Gillette commanded a market share of 67.6 percent of the $3 billion dollar American market for shaving products and accessories. The next closest competitor, Schick, had an 18.1 percent share, and BIC, a French manufacturer of disposable razors, a 7.2 percent share. The balance of the market consisted of private label brands. Despite a slight downward trajectory in market growth due to fewer men shaving as often as in the past and the growing social acceptance of facial hair in the workplace, Gillette's strategy had worked for over one hundred years, and there was little reason to suspect that a similar plan would not lead to success in the future.

The experts at Gillette were wrong, however, and did not divine the power of e-commerce. Beginning in early 2012, a new entrant in the shaving market, online shave clubs, arrived in the market. The first actor in the online market was Dollar Shave Club (DSC). The company was founded on what they believed were two underlying frustrations with the market: replacement blades were often locked at retail outlets and difficult to obtain, plus they were expensive. The CEO of Santa Monica, California based DSC, Michael Dubin, released a YouTube video in 2012 to introduce the company and claimed it could provide razors and blades at a fraction of the price and provide just as good, if not better, shaves. The video went viral within days, and Gillette learned of the video from its own employees. DSC used edgy tag lines, such as "Our Blades Give You a Great F***ing Shave," and "A Great Shave for a Few Bucks." DSC was targeting the male, 18 to 45 year-old market and assumed, correctly, that this segment was quite accustomed to buying a myriad of products online. The premise behind the club was to provide a lower-priced product and maximize customer convenience. The operating principles were simple: a customer chooses between a monthly $3, $6, or $9 plan, his or her credit card is charged, and the blades are delivered once a month. Trips to a retail store are eliminated.

Gillette's initial reaction to DSC was very dismissive. They believed their strategy of providing a stream of premium-priced products and getting customers to "trade-up" was unassailable. In March 2012, just after the release of the initial DSC YouTube video, Gillette spokesman Damon Jones said, "We became aware of Dollar Shave Club due to the internet buzz. However, we are not worried about losing market share, in part, because other subscription-based companies have tried and failed. If you want to spend 10 bucks a month, we have Gillette products available at all those price points." Despite their initial bravado, Gillette's share of the American shaving market had declined to 59.6% by the end of 2015, a drop of 8 points or nearly $250 million in revenue. They had clearly missed the transformative power of e-commerce due to their institutionalized mental model and unchanging strategy.

Online shave clubs are now a fixture on the American shaving scene. In 2015, online shave clubs accounted for 11.1 percent of the entire market, from being non-existent four years earlier. Total sales in this segment are over $330 million, with DSC accounting for two-thirds of this total. DSC's model has been copied by others, and there are now many DSC alternatives, such as Harry's Shave Club, Select Shave, and Dorco Shave Club. To combat the growth of DSC and other rivals,

Gillette now touts the longevity of their blades, continues to provide a plethora of new products to the market, and even began its own online shave club in 2014 but did not initially discount the price of their blades. Gillette also filed a lawsuit in December 2015 against DSC for patent infringement, even though DSC uses a contract manufacturer to fabricate their blades.

Gillette's mental model and experiential frame handicapped their strategic decision making and failed to allow for consideration of changes in their market. The company assumed customers would pay ever-increasing prices for razors and replacement blades—a tried and true strategy that had been successful for over one hundred years. Unaccounted for in their mental model were growing customer frustrations with obtaining blades—many display cases have subsequently been unlocked—and pricing. Additionally, the Gillette mental model did not envision new channels, such as e-commerce, for obtaining shaving products. Gillette will continue to be a dominant force in the American shaving market, but it will occupy a smaller space than it did in 2011, before the arrival of online shave clubs.

As a postscript, in April 2017, Gillette began slashing prices of its premium products and aggressively promoting its less expensive product offerings. Additionally, it changed the structure of their online shave club by discounting products, thereby creating less of a price differential with their competition. Time will tell whether these belated responses will stop defections to other online shave clubs and allow Gillette to recover lost market share.

CHAPTER SEVEN

Trust

The ability to establish, grow, extend, and restore trust is the key professional and personal competency of our time.

–Stephen M.R. Covey, author and
CEO of CoveyLink Worldwide

The Concept

To review key lessons so far, Perceptive Leaders build the organization's decision making skills by promoting diversity of thought, encouraging the use of devil's advocates and considering a range of alternatives. These leaders effectively manage uncertainty by creating an environment in the organization where team members can demonstrate productive paranoia and by ensuring staff feel free to say, "I don't know what the future holds, and this force is an uncertainty." However, if people in the organization do not feel safe in expressing their beliefs candidly, then none of these conditions can be met.

Perceptive Leaders know that these conditions rely on the existence of **Trust** throughout the organization. Stephen M.R. Covey, in his book *The Speed of Trust,* describes trust in this way: "Contrary to what most people believe, trust is not some soft, illusive quality that you either have or you don't: rather, trust is a pragmatic, tangible, actionable asset that you can create." This topic has been explored by many different authors, and we present three, including Covey, to emphasize the importance that thought leaders assign to trust. First, we offer a compelling example.

Alan Mulally was hired as CEO of Ford Motor Company in November 2006 with the explicit task of turning around the embattled company. A widely-reported first few weeks highlighted Mulally's commitment to building trust among his leadership team. As reported in a *Wall Street Journal* article at the end of 2006, Mulally's first executive team meeting revealed that the business unit heads were not forthcoming with information to the other executives, especially information regarding poor results. Mulally demanded that in their second meeting, he wanted the full set of data from each business unit head—good or bad. The next week in the meeting, only one leader gave an honest, *negative* report on performance. The other executives, according to reports, were aghast and anticipated a horrific response. Some sources even reported the other executives were contemplating when the leader would be fired. Instead,

Mulally applauded the executive, exclaiming "Great visibility!" After that meeting, the executive team members became much more supportive of one another, and more importantly became much more effective in solving major business issues as a team. They trusted that Mullaly would not penalize them for honestly sharing bad news.

Researchers have studied teams, different types of trust, and leaders who create a positive culture for trust. Stephen M.R. Covey, the son of Stephen Covey (who authored *Seven Habits of Highly Effective People*), wrote one of the more practical books on trust called *The Speed of Trust*. Covey makes a strong business case for trust and even argues that there are tangible economic benefits of trust and, conversely, real costs to distrust. While the book covers many types of trust, relationship trust is the most important for Perceptive Leaders. Covey identified 13 behaviors for relationship trust, and a few are most relevant for this discussion.

- Talk straight—be willing to give the full truth.

- Demonstrate respect and, even in dissent, show personal respect for others' opinions.

- Create transparency by demonstrating there are no hidden agendas.

- Confront reality and reward productive paranoia.

- Listen first and encourage diversity of thought before giving your point of view.

One of the most widely used frameworks around team dynamics and the relationship among team members is a model developed by Patrick Lencioni, business management consultant, and presented in several of his books including *Overcoming the Five Dysfunctions of a Team*. Lencioni asserts that the absence of trust is the foundational reason for dysfunctional teams. His work focuses on team trust and the willingness of a leader to be vulnerable, particularly around fears and weaknesses. This aligns with Covey's behaviors around talking straight and creating transparency.

Finally, business consultant Kim Scott recently published a book called *Radical Candor: Be a Kick-Ass Boss Without Losing Your Humanity*.

One of Scott's main premises is that leaders need to demonstrate to their team members that they care personally about their direct reports and should also be willing to talk candidly to them when providing feedback. She calls this *radical candor,* and our experience validates that when radical candor is present, employees feel there is a safe zone to provide diversity of thought and productive paranoia. Indeed, psychological safety, courageous conversations, and a culture of candor are all common phrases that have made their way into the management lexicon.

How important is trust? A boutique professional services firm was originally founded by two partners. This firm has a unique set of services and is highly regarded in that field. Top talent is continuously interested in joining this firm. The firm eventually grew to 35 people with five partners. These five partners are very close personally and professionally. They have no problem presenting diverse views in their partnership meetings but always know in the end they are like family. Not surprisingly, the top non-partner performers want to continue to grow and move forward professionally, with a potential future path to partnership. Recently the five current partners were faced with a dilemma—one of the highest performing, most talented principals was pushing for a partnership timeframe. However, there were a few issues around trust, particularly with other team members. This principal was threatening to leave the firm and possibly take clients if he wasn't given a partnership path. Ultimately, the five partners felt that the firm's differentiator was not the talent they could attract, but the trust among the partners. They felt if the trust was disrupted, the firm's competitive advantage would be gone. The principal was not given a path to partnership and ultimately left the firm. The firm is thriving.

What Should I Do as a Perceptive Leader to Build Trust across My Organization?

- As a leader, model the behavior you would like to see in your employees: in other words, walk the talk. If you are requesting an action or behavior from one of your team members, be sure you are ready to do the same.

- Be consistent in your treatment, behaviors, and actions.

- Build radical candor. Let people know that you offer a psychological safety zone. Call out good behavior as well as counter-productive behavior.

- Ensure that your team members really know and believe you care about them, about the work, and about their well-being.

Case Study

Abraham Lincoln and the American Civil War—Part II

Key Points

- Abraham Lincoln's decision to build a cabinet that ensured diversity of thought was presented in Chapter Two. This case explains the importance of trust in building a *functioning* diverse cabinet.

- Lincoln proved himself to be someone his cabinet members could trust through his humility, sincerity, and willingness to give credit to others.

- Not only did his cabinet members trust him, but Lincoln was able to build trust with key military leaders, especially General Grant. He demonstrated this trust by showing his faith in Grant's abilities.

- Lincoln is considered one of our greatest Presidents because of his accomplishments. Without building the trust of his cabinet, his military leadership, and the soldiers, his accomplishments would not have been possible.

The Story

Lincoln's decision making process was extremely deliberative. He would often listen to discussion among his cabinet without uttering a word, then announce his decision. Other times he would announce his decision, then encourage candid discussion. Lincoln was sometimes criticized in the national press for equivocating on issues, but on closer examination it appears he was waiting for just the right moment to publically announce a decision. His cabinet would often not agree with him, or each other, and held diverse points of view. However, all members appreciated his political acumen, intelligence, and compassion. They trusted Lincoln and ultimately supported his decisions.

You cannot have diversity of thought if you do not build trust. How did Abraham Lincoln build trust? First, the strength of his character and personal attributes, primarily his kindness, humility, humanity, and sincerity were quickly apparent to his former rivals. They swiftly realized that he was a unique man. Second, Lincoln spoke with candor and a homespun sense of self-deprecating humor—a quality often lacking in nineteenth-century politicians. Finally, Lincoln's unwavering devotion to restoration of the Union, not personal glory or gain, exhibited and reinforced his personal qualities.

On March 5th, his first day in office, President Lincoln was notified that Fort Sumter was running short of supplies. The South had already occupied many Federal coastal forts and installations. Lincoln's decision was whether to send a resupply ship or evacuate the garrison. He gathered his cabinet and asked each of them to provide a written response on their recommended course of action. Montgomery Blair was the lone member of his staff to recommend sending a resupply ship, with Chase equivocating. The other five cabinet members advised evacuation. Blair believed retention of Fort Sumter would rally southern Unionists to the Northern cause, while the other members thought it would provoke war. Lincoln's solution was a stroke of political genius.

He decided to notify Governor Pickens of South Carolina that he was sending an unarmed resupply ship to the fort. In essence, Lincoln had devised a "heads I win, tails you lose" situation for the South—the Union would retain the fort or the South would fire the first shots of the war. Jefferson Davis ordered artillery to fire upon the resupply ship and fort on April 12, 1861. Fort Sumter was bombarded for 33 hours and surrendered on April 14th. War was declared by both sides and four more states (Virginia, North Carolina, Tennessee, and Arkansas) seceded and joined the Confederacy. After the surrender of Fort Sumter, all members of the cabinet rallied to support Lincoln's decision.

Emancipation and abolition of slavery was an issue foremost in Lincoln's mind in early 1862. He saw that Confederate armies used slaves to build trenches and fortifications, drive supply wagons, and provide labor for many camp tasks. By having slaves conduct this type of labor, it freed white soldiers to fight. Lincoln recognized that slaves were a war resource and labor pool for the South, but he also believed that the institution was morally wrong. He was confronted by a problem with the Border States of Delaware, Maryland, Kentucky, and Missouri. These were states that had stayed with the Union, yet still practiced slavery. If Lincoln were to emancipate the slaves, he feared these states would secede. Nevertheless, by the summer of 1862 Lincoln read a draft of his decision on the matter to the cabinet and asked for comment. He believed that he held constitutional authority to order emancipation in states which were in rebellion due to his war powers, but not in those states where slavery was practiced, yet remained in the Union—the Border States.

Lincoln's cabinet was startled by his decision. Stanton and Bates supported him and believed that he should immediately issue the proclamation. Welles and Smith were silent and later confessed to serious reservations and unpredictable results. Blair was opposed and believed that the Border Sates would secede. Chase, the most anti-slavery member of the cabinet, surprisingly predicted disorder and advocated an incremental approach. Chase harbored designs on the 1864 Republican nomination and felt that Lincoln had undercut "his" issue. Seward was not opposed, but predicted disorder in the South. He feared that England and France would use the opportunity enter the war as a result. He advised Lincoln to wait until the military situation was in the North's favor—"until the eagle of victory takes his flight" and then Lincoln could "hang your proclamation about his neck." Lincoln heeded Seward's advice. His decision was to issue a preliminary Emancipation Proclamation in September 1862, after the major Union victory at Antietam. The Proclamation would become effective on January 1, 1863, if rebelling states did not return to the Union. Additionally, the Emancipation Proclamation did not apply to those states where slavery was practiced, but not in rebellion—the Border States. President Lincoln had solicited the opinions of his cabinet and incorporated their suggestions into his final decision. All the cabinet supported the final version of the Emancipation Proclamation, because they trusted Lincoln's deliberative decision making process.

The Emancipation Proclamation also enabled the recruitment of blacks into the Union Army. President Lincoln had been asked by Edwin Stanton in early 1862 for permission to enlist and arm black soldiers in the Union Army. As Union armies advanced, increasing numbers of escaped slaves were entering their lines. The ex-slaves were fed, clothed, and used as paid laborers, but arming them was a step Lincoln was not prepared to take in early 1862. He wanted to retain the loyalty of the Border States. Both Stanton and Chase supported enlisting blacks, but other members of the cabinet, particularly Bates, Blair, and Smith, were strongly against the idea. Lincoln believed that more time was needed to for the public mindset to evolve and accept this measure. The Emancipation Proclamation provided him this opportunity since the Civil War was now about both union and abolition. The Emancipation Proclamation specifically stated that blacks "be received into the armed forces of the United States." Black regiments began forming in early 1863, the first being the famed 54th Massachusetts under the command of Colonel Robert Gould Shaw of Boston. The black regiments faced hardship and prejudice from their Northern compatriots but eventually gained their lasting respect. If captured by the Confederates, they were often executed. Despite these predations, by the end of the war 180,000 blacks had served in Union armies. The enlistment of black soldiers, an issue formerly dividing his cabinet, was eventually a decision that all his cabinet supported by mid-1863.

Abraham Lincoln and His Generals

Abraham Lincoln not only inspired trust in his cabinet and former political rivals, he also had the trust of the military. The primary Union army in the east was known as the Army of the Potomac. While Lincoln did not consider himself a "military man," he had an uncanny ability to understand strategy. He believed, correctly, that given its material and manpower advantage, the Union should exert simultaneous pressure on several fronts in order to achieve military victory over the Confederates. He recognized that the North would need to conduct an offensive war to reunite the country through force. Unfortunately, he had a succession of commanders who did not share this vision. The litany of weak generals in the east included McDowell, McClellan, Burnside, and Hooker. Finally, in June 1863, on the eve of the battle of Gettysburg, Lincoln appointed the last commander—General George G. Meade. General Meade would serve as the commander of the primary Union field army for the balance of the war.

The North also had competent generals during the Civil War, but they came from the western armies. The eventual star was Ulysses S. Grant. Grant was appointed commander of all Union armies in late 1863 and moved his headquarters east. He co-located his headquarters with Meade and the Army of the Potomac, primarily to insulate Meade from political interference from Washington. Lincoln trusted Grant with the immense responsibility for all Union armies because of his record of success in the west, particularly the Vicksburg campaign. Lincoln and Grant became an inseparable tandem for the balance of the war. In early 1864, Lincoln promoted Grant to the position of General-in-Chief or Lieutenant General—a 3-star general and the first since George Washington—a supreme signal of his trust in Grant. Lincoln would discuss his grand strategy with Grant. The politician and general believed in conducting simultaneous offensives on multiple fronts, something previous commanders neglected. This strategy exerted maximum pressure on the beleaguered southern armies and eventually won the war. Grant came to admire Lincoln's intellect, generosity, kindness, humanity, and strategic vision.

An incident in early April 1865 displays this mutual sense of trust. Grant had been forewarned early in his tenure as General-in-Chief, by Secretary of War Stanton, not to discuss his specific plans with the president. According to Stanton, Mr. Lincoln was "so kind-hearted, so averse to refusing anything asked of him, that some friend would be sure to get from him all he knew." Grant heeded this advice and never discussed his specific plans with Lincoln. During the final week of the war, President Lincoln had moved to City Point, Virginia outside Petersburg, Virginia to be close to what he expected to be the final act of the war. Lincoln did not interject himself into the battle plan and let Grant conduct the operation. Grant did not tell Lincoln of his plans to capture Petersburg fearing that if he failed "it would have only added another to the many disappointments he [Lincoln] had been suffering for the past three years." After the city was captured, Grant asked Lincoln to meet him in Petersburg. Grant then revealed to Lincoln how he had executed the capture of the city and explained fully his plans to pursue the retreating enemy. The president then said to Grant: "Do you know, general, that I have had a sort of a sneaking idea for some days that you intended to do something like this." Trust between Lincoln and Grant was undoubtedly mutual.

1864 General Election

The 1864 general election presented Lincoln with an unexpected challenge. Some vocal Republicans felt he was not strong enough on promoting equality of the races, so they favored the Radical Republican Party. Democrats were divided between the Copperheads, who favored an immediate cessation of hostilities with the South, and the War Democrats who believed that the Civil War should be continued until its conclusion and victory over the Confederacy. In order to attract support from War Democrats and Border State politicians, the Republicans temporarily renamed themselves the National Union Party in mid-1864.

President Lincoln expected to be defeated as late as August 1864. The fighting in May and June had been unexpectedly bloody in Virginia. Additionally, Union military campaigns had stalled outside Atlanta and Richmond and Petersburg. Finally, Confederates had recently conducted a raid on Washington D. C. from positions in the Shenandoah Valley of Virginia. The political situation was grave for Lincoln, but the capture of Atlanta in September and victory over Confederate forces in the Shenandoah Valley during October provided Lincoln with the military successes that he needed to win reelection.

Lincoln soundly defeated his Democratic rival, George McClellan, in the November general election. Lincoln won 212 electoral votes, 22 states, and 55 percent of the popular vote. McClellan, the former commander of the Army of the Potomac, won 3 states and 22 electoral votes. One of the greatest demographic victories for Lincoln was the soldier vote. This was one of the first times that absentee voting was used for an American presidential election. Lincoln was loved and admired by Union soldiers because of his sympathy, compassion, and kindness. He won 78 percent of the soldier vote—a much larger percentage than the popular vote as a whole. The soldiers trusted him and wanted to continue prosecuting the war to its conclusion as evidenced by their overwhelming support.

Lincoln's Assassination and Lessons Learned

Lincoln's second inaugural address on March 4, 1865 began with one of his most memorable quotes—"with malice toward none, with charity for all." Ironically, Lincoln was assassinated less than six weeks after uttering these words. Peace was declared on April 9, 1865, Lincoln was shot on April 14th and died on April 15th. The Nation was in shock, Grant was inconsolable, and even General Robert E. Lee mourned. Secretary of State Seward, who was also a target of assassination the evening Lincoln was shot, was not initially told of Lincoln's death. His doctors did not believe he could withstand the shock. Seward knew that Lincoln was dead and told his hospital attendant that "if he had been alive he would have been the first to call on me." His attendant reported that Seward lay upon his back with "great tears coursing down his gashed cheeks" with the knowledge that his trusted friend was dead. Abraham Lincoln was trusted and admired by the nation, longtime friends, political opponents, and even former enemies.

Abraham Lincoln's life story befits a character in a Greek tragedy. He was born into humble beginnings on the edge of the frontier. With minimal formal education, he improved himself and through self-education became a lawyer and later politician. He lost more elections than he won. Additionally, he lost three of four children before they entered adulthood. These personal heartbreaks did not dampen his ambition to serve others. Lincoln's deep reservoir of personal qualities—intelligence, humanity, humility, kindness, compassion—inspired trust in others. In turn, his subordinates, both in his cabinet and the military, trusted him.

CHAPTER EIGHT

Internal Conditions

I came to see, in my time at IBM, that culture isn't just one aspect of the game, it is the game.

–Louis Gertzner, former CEO of IBM

The Concept

C hapter Five discussed the foundational capability of Perceptive Leaders to be able to effectively evaluate the external landscape of the organization. In the same way, leaders must be mindful of the **Internal Conditions**, since they have much more control of the internal environment.

David Nadler and Michael Tushman, two organizational theorists, developed the Congruence Model as a tool to identify performance issues within an organization, and it serves as a useful model to explore internal conditions. The Congruence Model features four elements that interact in an organization: the culture, the work itself, the people, and the structure of the organization. A further interpretation of the Congruence Model, espoused by many culture experts, argues that culture and structure in particular must be congruent or aligned with the corporate strategy to have successful strategy implementation. A famous quote about organizational culture from management guru Peter Drucker states, "Culture eats strategy for breakfast every time." Culture is widely recognized today as a key driver of organizational success, and in the view of IBM's former CEO, Louis Gertzner, the most important driver.

An example from the professional services industry illustrates the power of culture in implementing strategy. A large professional services firm was interested in new forms of revenue streams. The organization consisted of four business units or service areas that operated in silos, even though each business unit often served the same corporate client. On occasion, the senior partners from several of the business units would collaborate and develop a business solution for a client that did not fit neatly into any one business unit. The firm's senior partners realized they had a potential new revenue stream: cross-unit solutions for a corporate client. The firm decided upon a strategic initiative to build an "innovation incubator" that would explore cross-unit solutions in an innovative environment. The senior partners chose their most talented junior partners and asked them to join the innovation incubator for six months.

Most of the selected junior partners were not interested. Why? The structure of the organization's reward system was based on billable hours, and six months in an innovation incubator would not provide any client time. In other words, this new strategy and the current structure were not aligned. So, the senior partners decided upon a remedy where the junior partners would be made "whole" financially with discretionary funds. The structure became better aligned with the strategy—problem solved! Unfortunately, the junior partners were still not interested in the position and, in fact, were being advised by their senior partner mentors to stay away, far away, from that assignment. Again, why? The culture in this professional services firm was very client-focused, and the most admired partners, those promoted to the most senior levels, were the partners who had strong client relationships. Six months away from clients would be a career buster. The firm ultimately abandoned the incubator initiative, one that made perfect sense strategically, because *the culture was not aligned.*

Each of the four elements in the Congruence Model is complex and warrants its own field of study. For the purposes of building the capabilities of a Perceptive Leader who must lead in a VUCA environment, this chapter concentrates on the element of culture, and more specifically building an appropriate organizational culture that encourages adaptability.

Many formal definitions of corporate culture exist in the literature. Harvard professor Boris Groysberg and a group of colleagues conducted an exhaustive literature review of culture studies and presented their results in 2018 in the *Harvard Business Review*. The authors found four common themes across the literature:

- Culture is a group phenomenon with shared behaviors, values, and assumptions.

- Culture is pervasive, living in all levels of the organization.

- Culture is enduring, built over time and difficult to change in a short period of time.

- Culture is implicit, almost a "silent language."

In another study presented in *Harvard Business Review* in March 2015, the researchers identify best practices of companies that are successful in implementing strategy ("When Strategy Execution Unravels and What to Do About It"). One of their findings postulates organizations with a culture that rewards not only performance, but also agility, have better success in implementing strategy. Stated differently, organizations with a culture of agility, with shared behaviors and values supporting the ability to quickly adapt, were more successful.

Before exploring aspects of a culture of agility, we want to acknowledge that the term agility is currently associated with the many different "agile" methodologies being promoted by various consulting groups. Our definition of agility is more generic: the ability of an organization to adapt quickly to changes. Common words used in business lexicon today are the ability to *pivot*, to be *flexible*, to *adapt*, or to be *nimble*. Organizations seem to pick one of these to represent this capability around changing quickly in response to volatility in either external or internal conditions.

General Stanley McChrystal makes a strong case for a culture of agility in his book, *Team of Teams*, an accounting of his time leading NATO forces in Afghanistan and Iraq. McChrystal found that the traditional command and control structure of the military was inadequate in fighting the small and nimble forces of the enemy. He emphasized the need to create a group of small adaptable teams that were empowered to make decisions on the ground, while still maintaining a shared consciousness or commander's intent.

Perceptive Leaders understand their very important role in creating the right internal conditions to build a culture of agility. In fact, in many ways this entire handbook on *leading in an uncertain environment* is a roadmap for developing capabilities for agility. Lessons from previous and future chapters that promote a culture of agility include:

- Be clear about the **purpose** or commander's intent (Chapter One)

- Seek diversity of thought to combat the effects of **experiential frames** (Chapter Two)

- Reward the devil's advocate who provides **contrary views** (Chapter Four)

- Monitor the **external landscape** continuously (Chapter Five)

- Encourage **productive paranoia** (Chapter Six)

- Build **trust** and promote radical candor (Chapter Seven)

- Exhibit organizational **vigilance** (coming in Chapter Nine)

- Support **experimentation** (coming in Chapter Ten)

What Should I Do as a Perceptive Leader to Develop the Appropriate Internal Conditions to Promote a Culture of Agility?

- Understand your current organizational culture through a formal cultural audit, or employee engagement survey.

- Accept the results and determine the gaps between the aspirational culture of agility and your actual current culture within the organization.

- Most importantly, identify the gaps in culture, structure, people, and work that are needed to build adaptability.

- Allow empowered execution while ensuring clarity of shared consciousness.

Case Study

Robert Noyce and the Importance of Culture at Intel

Key Points

- The performance of an early employer of some of the Intel founders, Shockley Semiconductor Laboratories, was negatively impacted by its corporate culture. As a consequence, the company lost key talent, including the founders of Intel Robert Noyce and Gordon Moore.

- Embedded in the story of their subsequent company, Intel, are examples of many of the capabilities listed as necessary for a culture of agility: diversity of thought, productive paranoia, monitoring the external landscape, organizational vigilance, and experimentation.

- At Intel, Robert Noyce helped to build a culture of agility with his management style: he was entrepreneurial and risk-taking, he rewarded individuality, and he did not micro-manage.

- Also at Intel, the "third employee" Andy Grove recognized the need to be productively paranoid for an organization to thrive, which contributed to the culture of agility by always challenging the current industry assumptions.

- The three Intel leaders did not micro-manage, but empowered their employees to make decisions, particularly around experimentation.

The Story

Success breeds complacency. Complacency breeds
failure. Only the paranoid survive.

–Andy Grove

Companies nurture a culture of agility for a variety of reasons. Financial reward or gain for the company or individuals is obvious, but there are more subtle reasons. The landscape of their competitive environment may be changing so rapidly that only by developing new products can they guarantee, hopefully, their future existence. Also, the leadership of the company may be extremely curious, for purely intellectual reasons, about new extensions of their current product line or fresh challenges.

The case of Intel is compelling because its leaders—Robert Noyce, Gordon Moore, and Andy Grove—inculcated a culture of agility within their organization from its inception in the early 1960s. By any imaginable measure they were successful, and the subsequent development of the integrated circuit and microprocessor were instrumental in enabling the personal computer, internet, telecommunications, and the personal electronics revolution to make a lasting impression upon not only the United States, but the world.

Background and Proto-History

The story of the integrated circuit and microprocessor dates to the immediate post-World War II years and the lowly transistor. The predecessor to the transistor, the vacuum tube, was used extensively in the late 1930s and during World War Two as the critical component in electronic devices, particularly radar and electronic warfare instrumentation. However, the tubes were large and fragile; therefore, the devices using them were not robust and were also extremely large and cumbersome. A semiconductor was needed that was insensitive to variation and climate, and could be miniaturized. One of the key scientists working on semiconductor theory at AT&T was William Shockley. In late 1947, Shockley, through a series of experiments, designed a device featuring three wires dipped in silicon crystals and salts which amplified the current from one of the wires by a factor of forty. Thus was born the transistor, which AT&T announced to the world in June 1948. The firm continued to make improvements over the next few years.

The military was extremely interested in the transistor and spent lavish sums on it in the early 1950s. The government also challenged AT&T's monopoly on a technology deemed to be critical to national security. As a result, Bell Labs decided to license the new technology to a variety of industries and the government. They reasoned that more income could be generated from royalties than producing transistors, a process for which they were ill-equipped to manage. Bell Labs continued to conduct research in the field and provide talented scientists and engineers to other companies. The transistor still faced a major hurdle to commercialization—the vacuum tube industry. The tube industry was controlled by eight major companies, among them Raytheon, RCA, Philco, Westinghouse, General Electric, and Sylvania. These companies were all producing transistors, in addition to vacuum tubes, by the mid-1950s. There were also newcomers without vacuum tube experience that were producing transistors, such as IBM, Hughes Aircraft, Motorola, Texas Instruments, and Honeywell. The semiconductor field was soon very crowded. Few of the major tube manufacturers saw the transistor as revolutionary; therefore, many of the smaller "non-tube" transistor manufacturers were more driven and nimble, and soon supplanted the tube giants in the semiconductor field.

William Shockley, who was a pioneer in the semiconductor field and shared the 1956 Nobel Prize for physics, became restless and left Bell Labs in the mid-1950s. Shockley approached Arnold Beckman, owner of his namesake scientific instrument company, for financial backing for a new semiconductor company—Shockley Semiconductor Laboratories, headquartered in Palo Alto, then Mountain View, California. Shockley had no problem hiring the best talent in the nation because of his renown, but he often clashed with his staff on his management style. He wished to banish secrecy, so everyone's salary was publically posted. He personalized problems, and also posted peer reviews. He had a consuming goal of developing a two-terminal, four-layer diode, which, while technically sophisticated, had few commercial prospects. His staff tried to get him to focus on silicon transistors, but Shockley refused. Shockley may have been brilliant, but his intellectual hubris masked a complete lack of management skills. As a result, the corporate culture at Shockley Semiconductor Laboratories became an impediment to the growth of the company. Eventually many of his most talented engineers, "the traitorous eight" as Shockley called them, left and established a new company, financed by Fairchild Camera & Instrument.

The Formation of Intel

Two of Shockley's most talented and brilliant employees were Robert Noyce and Gordon Moore. They both left Shockley as part of the "traitorous eight" in 1957. With a loan of $1.5 million, they founded Fairchild Semiconductor, a wholly owned subsidiary of Fairchild Camera and Instrument. Their story at Fairchild Semiconductor is explored in depth in the Vigilance Chapter. The final chapter of Noyce and Moore's days at Fairchild, and beginning of the Intel story, came in 1968. The CEO position at Fairchild Camera and Instrument was open and Noyce was deemed a logical choice, as he led the most profitable unit of the company. However, he was passed over. After this grave disappointment, Noyce joked to his good friend Moore that they should leave and start their own company, and that is exactly what they did. Noyce and Moore first named their new firm NM Electronics, then renamed it Integrated Electronics, and finally shortened it to Intel. While not recognized as a founder of Intel, Andy Grove joined the firm on the day it was incorporated and was its third employee, behind Noyce and Moore.

The "Intel Trinity" all had vastly different backgrounds, which provided an inherent promotion of diverse thought within the culture at Intel. Robert Noyce was born in 1927 in Burlington, Iowa. As a youngster, Noyce was instructed in the values of hard work, education, and frugality. He was an inquisitive and high-spirited boy, whose impetuous behavior often got him in trouble. His mother enrolled him in a college physics course as a high school student to provide him an outlet for his active intellect. Noyce attended and graduated from Grinnell College in Grinnell, Iowa. At Grinnell, Noyce developed an interest in transistors and was encouraged by his mentor, Dr. Grant Gale, to enroll in a doctoral program at MIT. Upon graduation from MIT, he accepted a job with Philco in Philadelphia, and his work on transistors quickly gained the attention of nationally known figures, such as William Shockley. Noyce was the leader of the group due to his engaging personality.

Gordon Moore's path to Shockley was similar to Noyce, but his interests were initially more academic and focused on electrical engineering. Born in 1929 in San Francisco, Moore began his studies at San Jose State and transferred to the University of California—Berkeley and earned his bachelor's degree in chemistry in 1950. He then moved to Caltech and earned a PhD in chemistry in 1953. From Caltech, Moore completed postdoctoral work at the Applied Physics Laboratory at Johns Hopkins from 1953 until 1956, when he left Hopkins and joined Shockley in late 1956. He was recognized very early as bright and a person interested in research, but he was much less rambunctious than Noyce. In 1965, while at Fairchild Semiconductor as the director of research and development, Moore was asked by an interviewer what would happen the next ten years in the industry. He postulated what became known as "Moore's Law"—that the number of transistors, capacitors, diodes, and resistors in an integrated circuit would continue to double every year, then after ten years double every two years. At the Intel start-up, Moore was the executive vice president and led the organization's innovation of specific products.

The final member of the "trinity" was Andy Grove, who met Noyce and Moore in 1963 when he joined Fairchild Semiconductor. Born in Hungary in 1936 into a middle-class Jewish family, Grove and his mother used false identification papers and were hidden by friends to escape Nazi persecution in 1944. His father was sent to a labor camp and only reunited with Andy and his mother after the war. He escaped Hungary in 1956 during the Hungarian Revolution and slipped over the border to Austria and subsequently in 1957 immigrated to the United States. Arriving penniless and barely able to speak English, Grove mastered the language and graduated in 1960 from the City College of New York with a bachelor's degree in chemical engineering. He matriculated to the University of California—Berkeley after graduation from CCNY and earned a PhD in chemical engineering in 1963. Grove joined Fairchild upon his graduation from Berkeley and worked for Moore as a researcher, becoming the assistant director of research and development, under Moore, in 1967. His initial job at Intel was director of engineering and most of his work over the years focused on streamlining, improving, and devising new manufacturing processes. Grove became a prolific author, and one of his most famous works was *Only the Paranoid Survive* published in 1996.

The Intel Corporate Culture

One attribute which quickly distinguished Intel from its competitors, besides its talented leadership, was its corporate culture. Central to this corporate culture was Noyce. He had a unique personality, an endearing management style, and sought solace in a variety of thrill-seeking hobbies. He was ambitious, competitive, extremely bright, confident, and frugal. He immersed himself in his work and was most comfortable when designing solutions to practical problems, rather than writing theoretical papers. As a manager, Noyce was a charismatic leader who inspired confidence and trust in his subordinates. He was entrepreneurial to the core, risk-taking, always sought to find better solutions to a problem, eschewed hierarchy while embracing informality, and saw worth in individual employees. He was a "big picture" thinker and avoided becoming embroiled in many of the administrative details of the company. This type of management style required strong administrative talent behind the scenes, and both Moore and Grove provided these skills.

One of the most important elements of the Intel corporate culture was the development of productive paranoia, not just in developing a constant stream of innovative solutions and products, but in how the company interacted with customers. Noyce sought to design products around customer needs, not requirements, by incrementally improving upon the inventions of others. He championed a creative, open, and collaborative process for innovation and experimentation. The integrated circuit depended upon the work of John Last and the planer process for making a uniform flat-surface silicon chip. The microprocessor was designed around the technical ideas of Ted Hoff, improvements in the acid dip test to increase yield, and the customer support of Frederico Faggin, but Noyce had the vision to support the IC project and establish a market for the product. He placed customer needs first and foremost. He may have received credit as the inventor of the integrated circuit and microprocessor, but the process was truly collaborative.

The Maturation Process

Intel continued to grow and became one of the most successful technology companies of the time. Then economic recession in 1974 forced Noyce to furlough 30 percent of the Intel workforce. Devastated by this action, Noyce resigned from daily operations at Intel in 1975 and became the Chairman of the Board—the public face of the company. Noyce resigned the chairmanship and became vice-chairman in 1979, devoting much of his time working for the semiconductor industry in their battle for worldwide supremacy with Japan. He scored numerous political victories as an industry lobbyist and member on congressional and presidential committees. He passed away in 1990 of a massive heart attack.

Robert Noyce may have been the initial creative engine at Intel, but Moore and Grove sustained the initial success. After Noyce's departure, Moore and Grove, managed the daily operations at Intel. Their task was to change the management style at Intel from an entrepreneurial start-up to an ongoing business while continuing the pattern of innovative creativity. Moore became president in 1975 upon Noyce's resignation and held this position until 1979, when he was appointed CEO and chairman, again after Noyce resigned to work on behalf of the entire industry. The choice to replace him as president was Andy Grove. Moore held these dual roles until 1987, when he surrendered the CEO position to Grove, yet remained as chairman until 1997, when he then became chairman emeritus. Grove began his tenure as chairman and CEO in 1998 and held these dual roles until 2005, when he retired due to health concerns, yet was retained as a special advisor. Grove passed away in 2016.

The maturation process at Intel is both typical and unique in the electronics industry. The entrepreneurial and creative genius at the outset, Robert Noyce, left daily management of the company to others— Moore and Grove—who had leadership styles more complementary to creating an ongoing and maturing company. The result was the creation of the unrivaled market leader. Intel is typical of other technology companies, such as Microsoft and Apple, in this regard. What makes Intel unique is the continuity of its leadership and succession over the years. From 1968 until 2005, a period of thirty-seven years, at least one member, and often multiple members, of the original "trinity" held a company leadership role. The spirit of creation, productive paranoia, and agility begun by Noyce was continued by his successors.

Lessons Learned

This case is instructive for several reasons. First, many of the innovations in the field of electronics have been driven by the intellectual challenge and changes posed by the technology. The quest to improve upon existing designs and provide something better for the market began with Shockley and continued with Intel. Noyce, Moore, and Grove were fascinated by the technology and its possibilities and regarded future innovation as a supreme intellectual challenge. Second, the Intel leadership was masterful in creating a culture of agility—one that supported diversity of thought, productive paranoia, trust, and experimentation—which led to great commercial success. Finally, this productive paranoia led to a need for the ability to "see around corners," which is extensively explored in the next chapter case study.

CHAPTER NINE

Vigilance

Those who have knowledge, don't predict. Those who predict, don't have knowledge.

–Lao Tzu, Chinese Philosopher

The Concept

In today's ever changing business environment, the pursuit of an accurate prediction of the future is often folly, as Lao Tzu suggests. One of the most important organizational capabilities to manage uncertainties is **Vigilance**—the ability to anticipate changes by dynamically monitoring key uncertainties. Perceptive Leaders acknowledge what they do not know (they can distinguish between certainties and uncertainties) and then determine a way to scan for early indicators of change. Vigilance is the natural next step after explicitly identifying key uncertainties or known unknowns (Chapter Five) and challenging the organizational mental model with productive paranoia (Chapter Six).

As discussed in previous chapters, leaders have many challenges that make it difficult for them to admit they do not have complete knowledge of a particular subject. The overconfidence bias, organizational mental models, and a lack of diversity of thought all discourage a leader from saying the words "I don't know." Yet a Perceptive Leader *must* build this capability to be able to look for leading indicators, not lagging indicators, of change, which requires the acceptance of not knowing.

To understand the concept of early indicators, let's return to the example of the lean process from Chapter Five on the external landscape. The lean process focuses on eliminating variability when possible and controlling the variability that cannot be eliminated. Engineers try to manage the variability with a quality control (QC) process that uses QC Charts.

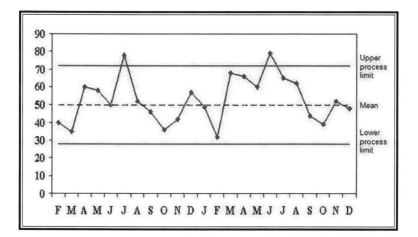

The sample control chart above illustrates the type of information provided by these charts. We are not given the units of measure on the vertical axis in the chart, but the dotted line represents the target value, 50, within the process. The upper process limit and the lower process limit represent the variability tolerance. For example, the target value for this process is 50 but the process can still be "in control" if the monthly number stays within 20 points higher or lower, or between 30 and 70. In this chart, the monthly value fell OUT of a normal range in July and then the next June.

Strategic early indicators act similarly to these "out of control" values illustrated in the July and June points. The points may or may not indicate a permanent shift in the process, but serve as weak signals of change. Just as in a manufacturing process, Perceptive Leaders want to be vigilant and look for early indicators of change, particularly around high-impact uncertainties. They also encourage their employees to do the same, which is illustrated in the story below.

Several years ago Kathy was discussing the uncertain environment facing retail banks with a woman who had served as a loan officer ten years prior to our conversation. They both agreed that financial services institutions were in danger of major disruption, but many of their leaders were failing to admit the uncertainties. Kathy and her colleague attributed this "blind eye" to the fact that banking had been a fairly stable industry until the last few years. The woman related a story that was very instructive. When she formerly held a position as a loan officer in a retail branch, on her day off she had gone shopping at a popular store. After perusing the merchandise she proceeded to the counter to pay for her selections. The cashier asked if she wanted to apply for a store credit card and receive 15 percent off on her purchases that day. Kathy's colleague declined due to lack of time and the woman behind the counter told her it would literally take 60 seconds with a valid driver's license.

The next day when the colleague was working at the bank, one of the bank's best customers came to her office. The customer was a long-standing customer of thirty years, with mortgages, a small business loan, and three accounts with the bank. The customer asked to register for a $1000 overdraft protection plan on one of his checking accounts. The loan officer had to tell him that approval would take *two weeks*! The loan officer approached her boss and said "I just received an offer for a $1000 line of credit from our local clothing store and that store knows nothing about my credit rating. One of our A+ clients has asked for $1000 overdraft protection, and we have mountains of concrete data showing his excellent credit rating, and our client must wait two weeks?" Her boss shrugged and said, "Sorry—company policy." He simply could not see the relevance of the customer's retail experience in the store to the customer's checking account and was seemingly unwilling to elevate the situation to the policy makers within the bank.

Perceptive Leaders **want** employees to make the connection between the retail clothing store and the retail banking services. They also recognize that the early indicators of change are often seen by staff members who are closest to the external environment—those working directly with clients or customers—and not the leaders at the top of the corporate ivory tower. And yet, organizations reward those employees based on short term metrics, not on their ability and willingness to be vigilant.

Recently Kathy had an interesting discussion with a senior leader around hiring for this capability of vigilance. He was convinced that agility is one of the most important competencies for organizations in the future—particularly large, well established organizations—and understood that vigilance is necessary to anticipate areas for agility. He asked a very compelling question. "Who should I hire to build this capability? What kind of employee do I want?" Kathy considered the loan officer's story and many other examples of people with whom she have worked who make those connections on a regular basis. She concluded that a primary characteristic is intellectual curiosity. That conclusion was validated in the *Harvard Business Review* in October 2018 in an article titled, "The Business Case for Curiosity." The authors make the case that leaders must not only become more curious themselves, but need to develop their staff to be more curious and to determine a way to reward curiosity.

In summary, Perceptive Leaders want to be vigilant, and want employees to be vigilant as well, so they can spot *leading* indicators, not *lagging* indicators, of change.

What Should I Do as a Perceptive Leader to Build Organizational Vigilance?

- Recognize that accurate prediction of the future is often impossible.

- As mentioned before, be willing to say "I don't know" as a leader and be explicit about known unknowns with your staff.

- Seek information on leading indicators not just in your organization's immediate external environment, but also beyond your own market, country, or industry.

- Encourage intellectual curiosity in your team members and reward them when they identify early indicators of change.

Case Study

Vigilance at Intel

Key Points

- Robert Noyce and Gordon Moore were initially successful at Fairchild Semiconductors, but eventually left because the parent company, Fairchild Camera and Instrument, became a barrier due to its inability to recognize the importance of vigilance in monitoring the external environment.

- Specifically, Fairchild Camera and Instrument missed both the change in manufacturing technology and the change in employee compensation models.

- By contrast, when Noyce and Moore founded Intel, they ensured not only a culture of agility but specifically emphasized the need for vigilance within the organization.

- Intel leaders recognized the interest in more innovative products and encouraged an emphasis on customer needs, not just requirements.

- Intel leaders also saw that potential customers were not limited to one Japanese company, or to IBM alone, but were willing to break with industry standards to pursue other sources of revenue.

The Story

In the previous chapter we learned about the culture at Intel and how this culture of agility led to incredible organizational success. Embedded in this culture of agility was specifically the vigilance of the leaders in identifying changes in the external environment—which supported the entrepreneurial spirit within the ranks.

Fairchild Semiconductors

Two of the most talented and brilliant employees at Shockley Semiconductor were Robert Noyce and Gordon Moore. They both left Shockley as part of the "traitorous eight" in 1957. With a loan they founded Fairchild Semiconductor, a wholly owned subsidiary of Fairchild Camera and Instrument. Noyce was recognized as the leader of the group, and he quickly realized that the "winners" in the industry had to master low-cost and high volume manufacture of transistors and get new products to market quickly. Moore was the director of technological innovation at the company. Rapid fabrication was key because the raw materials, essentially sand and wire, were very inexpensive. Fairchild had mastered the planer process for rapidly manufacturing transistors. The process began with a sketch of the transistor which was then photographed and miniaturized into a tiny transparency, with multiple transparencies for each layer of the circuit. Simultaneously, a tubular silicon crystal was sliced into thin pieces and each wafer was coated with a photosensitive material. When a strong ultraviolet light was fired through the transparencies and onto the coated wafer, the unexposed areas were projected onto the wafer. These areas were then etched away with acid and subsequently plated with a metal conductor or insulator, thus completing the circuit. One of the other innovations attributable to Noyce and Moore at Fairchild was the integrated circuit. Essentially, the IC had multiple linked transistors on a single slice of silicon. The process of miniaturization occupied much of their time at Fairchild. Moore was seen as the technical genius, and Noyce the consummate leader who was bright, had a vision for innovative products, eschewed hierarchy, and was the glue that bound the "traitorous eight" together.

By 1965, however, Fairchild had begun to show signs of weakness. Competition was becoming more pronounced, and they were losing market share, while internal squabbles had arisen between the engineers in California and management in New York. Also, there was a culture clash between the parent and subsidiary. Fairchild Camera and Instrument was an old- line, conservatively managed company. A new chip manufacturing process was being developed called MOS or metal-oxide semiconductor technology. This new process was beginning to appear at some competitors, but these early indicators were ignored by Fairchild Headquarters over the objections of the group at Fairchild Semiconductor. Subsequently, departures and raiding of key talent from Fairchild Semiconductor began in 1966. In order to retain talent, Noyce suggested offering employees stock options, a practice he recognized as a potential industry norm as it was becoming popular within the industry. This incentive was also summarily rejected by Fairchild Headquarters. The talent drain continued, and the parent company failed to recognize what became lagging indicators of change in the industry.

Early Innovation Breakthroughs at Intel

After leaving Fairchild and founding Intel, Noyce and Moore's first objective was to develop an integrated circuit capable of functioning as a memory device, and which would be less expensive to produce than magnetic core memory devices. The first three years at Intel were highly productive, and the company quickly established itself as the primary innovative force in the industry with products such as the 1103 chip, which proved to be a better chip than the magnetic core device. Intel also developed a microprocessor for a Japanese company named Busicom where a single logic chip performed the functions of multiple specialized chips by offloading many instructions to a memory chip. Intel anticipated there might be demand outside of Busicom for the technology, so the company pursued an agreement from Busicom to sell this technology for other electronic applications. Noyce then tirelessly promoted the microprocessor within the industry. In 1971, Intel developed the 4004 microprocessor, which became the first commercially available unit on the market.

The leaders at Intel recognized some signals that customers needed smaller, faster chips, so the quest for miniaturization and more powerful memory drove the company's efforts. Intel became a public corporation in October 1971. Its IPO was for 350,000 shares of stock priced at $23.50 each. The total capital raised was $8.22 million, which was a huge sum at the time, but a rounding error today. Intel designed the 8080 chip in 1974, which became the standard chip for computers, and in 1979 Intel convinced IBM to use its 8086 chip in its PCs. The partnership with IBM and personal computing was the context for unimaginable growth in the 1980s.

The boom in the personal computer market in the 1980s presented Intel, as well as their competitors, with great opportunities. Intel became the unrivaled industry frontrunner as the leadership anticipated the rise of "IBM clone" PCs. In 1986 they signed an agreement with Compaq, the leading manufacturer of IBM clone PCs, to use the 386 chip in its machines. Intel, specifically Andy Grove, also decided to "single-source" the 386 chip, which broke with industry tradition. Previously, Intel would have the fabrication of its chips done under contract with other chip manufacturers. In the 1980s Intel built several other fabrication facilities, and made all the chips itself, rather than having them made under licensing agreements with others, which were often competitors. After the x86 series of microprocessors in the 1980s came the Pentium series in the 1990s and the Core series in the 2000s. By 1992 Intel had become the largest chip manufacturer, by revenue, in the world, and they have held this position ever since. Intel products are used in 73.3 percent of all personal computers worldwide and they have an 80.4 percent share of the laptop / mobile PC segment, as of 2017.

Vigilance within the Intel Culture

Clearly Intel and its leaders paid close attention to leading indicators in the semiconductor industry and, more broadly, in the technology world. They were also able to inculcate this ability to "see around corners" and anticipate changes within the industry, because of the storied Intel culture. For example, Noyce believed that knowledge trumped hierarchal authority and encouraged his employees to push creative ideas further by focusing on the customer perspective. Intel employees developed a passion to deliver what customers needed, even before the customer realized that they had such a need. The watchword was to solve customer needs, not just requirements. Noyce and his colleagues observed that innovative and interesting products were becoming more appealing than established and safe ones.

The case of IBM and the personal computer is illustrative. IBM came to Intel with a problem and a set of requirements. Intel delivered an integrated chip capable of performing the functions of several singular components. To understand those evolving consumer needs, Intel employees had to be attuned to consumer changes, particularly in the area of personal computing, to be successful.

Another reason to promote vigilance was to be able to remain competitive in a growing field. The leaders at Intel felt a constant challenge presented by their primary competition—the Japanese chip manufacturers. The competition was handsomely financed by their government, and the specter of an all-consuming corporate battle was the context of the relationship between Intel and their Japanese counterparts. The solution at Intel was to create an environment of hyper-vigilance where the only course of action to win this ultimate battle was to consistently and dynamically monitor the external environment and be prepared to create and market new products with an undying sense of urgency.

Finally, Noyce observed early in the evolution of the growing technology field that a work environment emphasizing innovation and experimentation would encourage frequent departure of key employees to "start-up" their own companies. This leading indicator of change in talent eventually became accepted practice in Silicon Valley.

Lessons Learned

The Intel leadership demonstrated a keen attention to early indicators in the external environment as they made decisions around technology development and potential customers, initially outside of Japan and then later outside of IBM. They also inculcated their culture of agility with a focus on external vigilance.

A final oft-told anecdote of Noyce's entrepreneurial leadership style and attention to the weak signals occurred in 1965 and ultimately led to a change in the pricing structure for the entire semiconductor industry. At an industry meeting, Noyce arose and said that the pricing for all integrated circuits the next year would be ***one dollar*** each. This level was well below standard industry pricing levels and even less than current manufacturing costs. His reasoning for such an audacious move was that within a year or two, the price would fall to one dollar anyway, so why not set the price where it would be in a year or two. This strategy would capture market share and customers before competitors could respond. Noyce recognized some critical leading indicators and was willing to act on these indicators before other players, providing Intel with a great competitive advantage.

CHAPTER TEN

Experimentation

An organization's ability to learn, and translate that learning into action rapidly, is the ultimate competitive advantage.

–Jack Welsh, former CEO of General Electric

The Concept

A very popular topic in organizational development today is the area of innovation. Indeed, companies like IDEO have built burgeoning consulting practices through helping organizations formalize the innovation process internally. Clay Christiansen wrote a best-selling book called *The Innovator's Dilemma* and built a theory around "innovative disruption." Many of these innovation models encourage **Experimentation** and a higher tolerance for failure.

Experimentation is also a key element of the lean process, which we have discussed in previous chapters. In the highly-touted Toyota Production System, for example, managers allow the manufacturing line employees to test new processes, with the premise that they are closest to the manufacturing lines and know best. Finally, experimentation is an important component in product development—marketers will ask "Will it play in Peoria?" to encourage pilots and focus groups.

Perceptive Leaders understand that the ability to experiment is critical not just for innovation, manufacturing process design, and product development, but also to manage uncertainty and build adaptability. Irving Wladawsky-Berger, an ex-IBM executive and contributor to *CIO Journal* of the *Wall Street Journal,* discussed the requirements for an innovation culture in a March 2, 2019 article titled "Fostering an Innovation Culture: Talent, Discipline and Leadership." He explained the need for disciplined experimentation in the following way: "Organizations that embrace experimentation are comfortable with uncertainty and ambiguity …. they experiment to learn rather than to produce an immediately marketable product or service." The author made the point that organizations need to emphasize the learning aspect of experimentation, which is completely aligned with managing uncertainty effectively.

Of course, actually encouraging experimentation in organizations is no easy task. First, even though many leaders claim to seek a higher tolerance for failure, anecdotal evidence shows that more established organizations have a harder time implementing a tolerance for failure because, quite frankly, failure is not rewarded. The emphasis must be on a desire for learning, for "test and learn" projects or rapid experiments as opposed to a "success/failure" project. The distinction is not just semantic. Perceptive Leaders say, "I want to learn something about my customer," "I want to learn something about my vendor," "I want to learn something about my process," or "I want to learn about this particular uncertainty" and then design an experiment motivated by the opportunity to gain knowledge.

The second barrier to experimentation is the organizational structure. In Chapter Eight on Internal Conditions, the Congruence Model was introduced and one of the four elements in this model is structure. Often organizations have such onerous processes around decision making and gaining "approval" for experiments that employees are discouraged from this important activity. The structure and bureaucracy are difficult to overcome.

General Stanley McCrystal discusses the structural challenge in his book, *Team of Teams*. General McChrystal commanded NATO forces in both Afghanistan and Iraq. The US military traditionally has had a hierarchical structure, and yet his forces were facing an enemy comprised of small and nimble teams. He knew he needed to change the structure of his force if his military was to have a chance of defeating the insurgents. He named this new structure a "team of teams." We encourage any Perceptive Leader to read this book, as it recounts an amazing case study of the congruence model. But one key element of the team of teams structure is what General McCrystal calls "empowered execution." He knew his teams needed to have the authority to act as they saw fit without a bureaucratic process of approval.

Managing uncertainty is challenging, and without the ability to experiment, to continuously learn about uncertainties, organizations will not be able to adapt or be agile. How does an organization determine areas for potential experimentation? One method we use with clients is to build a heat map of key strategic initiatives and key uncertainties. Consider the chart below:

Initiative	U1	U2	U3	U4	U5	U6
Initiative 1	Gray	Gray	Black	Gray	Gray	Black
Initiative 2	Gray	Black	Gray	Gray	Gray	Gray
Initiative 3	Black	Gray	Gray	Black	Gray	Gray
Initiative 4	Gray	Gray	Black	Gray	Black	Gray
Initiative 5	Gray	Gray	Black	Gray	Gray	Gray
Initiative 6	Gray	Gray	Gray	Gray	Gray	Gray

This chart illustrates a heat map for a particular business unit with six strategic initiatives and six key uncertainties. A black box indicates the success of the initiative is highly dependent upon the uncertainty, and a gray box designates little correlation.

By way of a more specific example, suppose a major initiative of a business school is to redesign the current MBA program curriculum, and two major uncertainties are the popularity of offering an online degree and the business skills that will be required in the future. Online learning is a method of delivery of the content, so the business school can assume there is not much dependence between the initiative and the uncertainty. However, the business skills needed in the future will have a huge impact on the curriculum.

Initiative	Online Learning	Business Skills Needed in the Future	Uncertainty 3
Redesign MBA Curriculum	Gray	Black	
Initiative 2			
Initiative 3			

If we return to the generic heat map, the leaders of the business unit can discern that for their particular strategy and strategic priorities,

Uncertainty 3 is quite important. A Perceptive Leader would then consider small bets or experiments around Uncertainty 3 to learn more about the uncertainty, to dynamically monitor the uncertainty (as discussed in the Vigilance chapter), or to potentially develop an adaptive approach to implementing the current initiatives.

In summary, in the pursuit of managing uncertainty effectively, Perceptive Leaders recognize that the impetus for experimentation is learning and adaptability, not necessarily innovation in isolation.

What Should I Do as a Perceptive Leader to Encourage Experimentation?

- Eliminate the word "failure" from your organizational vocabulary and instead use "Rapid Experiments" or "Test and Learn" or some other similar phrase that emphasizes learning, not necessarily innovation.

- Highlight instances of experimentation in a positive way, regardless of "outcome." Shine a spotlight on key learnings, independent of whether the experiment proved or disproved the hypothesis.

- Dedicate funds not just to innovation projects, but to "learning experiment" projects.

- Practice empowered execution.

- Use a heat map to determine possible areas for experimentation that supports your strategic priorities.

Case Study

The Evolution of the Tin Food Can

Key Points

- The development of the tin can is a classic example of innovation and the use of trial and error, or experimentation, to achieve a now ubiquitous product.

- There were many uncertainties the innovators faced in the years of the development. Rapid experimentation helped to contain the cost of testing and learning.

- Although there were many "failures," the development of the current tin can would not have been possible without the learnings that occurred in the trial and error process.

- Cobb Preserving seemingly made a "big bet" at the end, but one could argue they were just taking advantage of what had become a known known or certainty: the consumer rising demand for a sanitary can.

The Story

Experimentation, also known as trial-and-error development, has been a very common method for technological innovation. The creators of many life-changing products and processes of the late nineteenth and early twentieth centuries were independent inventors. These independent inventors, such as Edison, Tesla, Bell, Ford, and the Wright Brothers, were driven by solving a vexing problem, sometimes due to potential financial rewards, but more often because of a naturally inquisitive mind. They shared many common character traits: little formal education (Tesla was an exception), the desire to solve a problem or make an improvement to an existing product or process, a wish to increase efficiency, and maybe even to make a profit. Their process of invention was characterized by trial-and-error or empirical approaches. Independent inventors were often cash strapped and almost exclusively self-supporting and tended to work alone, or with a very limited number of colleagues. Products and processes, like the motion picture, alternating current power generation, the telephone, the automobile and mass production assembly line, and the airplane, are well-known and were created through a series of trials, failures, and experimentation. One lesser known, yet ubiquitous product, the modern tin food can, was also a product of the independent inventor, and achieved its current form through experimentation.

Early Nineteenth-Century Can Manufacturing

The genesis of the tin can dates to the French Revolution and the wars of Napoleon. In 1795, the French Society for the Encouragement of New Inventions, a department of the Ministry of the Interior, offered a prize of 12,000 francs for a practicable method of food preservation. The primary concern of the Society was providing the French Navy with provisions they could carry with them on deployments. In 1809 the prize was awarded to Nicolas Appert, a confectioner, pickler, wine-maker, brewer, chef, distiller, and army contractor. He had no scientific training, and his process of experimentation was characterized by trial-and-error or guesswork. Appert's "canning" process used sealed glass jars submerged in a bath of boiling water for various periods of time, depending upon what was being packed. He had concluded, from experimental observation, that prolonged exposure of products to air was the root cause of spoilage. However, the application of heat could preserve food in sealed containers, thereby negating the effects of air and prevent spoilage. His process was time consuming, and the price of his sealed containers very expensive. Nevertheless, the canning industry was born, with Appert recognized forevermore as the "Father of Canning."

Canning arrived in America several decades after its inception in Europe. In Boston, Englishman William Underwood established a firm in 1821, William Underwood and Company, which specialized in pickles, ketchup, sauces, fruit jams, and jellies, for primarily export markets in the West Indies, South America, and Asia. Underwood also packed milk, lobster, salmon, various fruits, and tomatoes for his local clients. At nearly the same time as Underwood, Thomas Kensett and his father-in-law Ezra Daggett, also Englishmen trained in the art of food preservation, began canning oysters, lobsters, and fish in New York City. Kensett moved his business to Baltimore in 1839 to take advantage of the ready availability of seafood: oysters, crabs, and fish, plus the accessibility of a wide variety of fruits and vegetables from the local community. Soon after his move to Baltimore, Kensett began using tin rather than glass when the costs and lack of supply for imported glass containers made the switch to a tin can an economic imperative. From his trials using tin canisters, soon shortened to tin cans, Thomas Kensett might be considered the founder of the tin can in America.

Effect of the American Civil War

The breakthrough event for popularization of the tin can was the American Civil War. It has been estimated that there had been 5 million tin cans sold in America on the eve of the Civil War in 1860. There were three contingent conditions for its subsequent rapid diffusion. First, a product with mass appeal was a requirement. Second, a convenient method of opening a can—the can opener—was essential. Finally, consumer demand, primarily in the Union, spiked during the War.

The first product with mass appeal, and not just considered a luxury item such as oysters, was condensed milk. Gail Borden experimented for much of the 1850s for a method that evaporated water from milk. He finally perfected his process and applied for, and received, a patent for his condensing process in 1856. Borden's condensed milk would become a favorite specialty item purchased by soldiers, primarily Union, during the War.

Gail Borden had created a canned product in the 1850s with the potential for mass appeal, but there was still no reliable and safe method for opening a tin can until the eve of the Civil War. Soldiers, sailors, explorers, miners, and pioneers had to attack tin cans with knives, bayonets, or a hammer and chisel. These rudimentary methods were

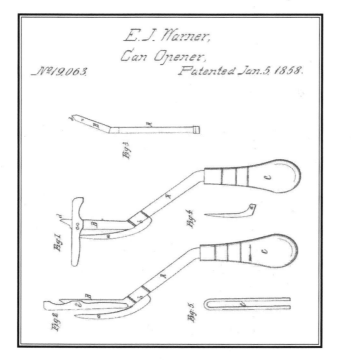

Diagram of Ezra Warner's Can Opener. U. S. Patent and Trademark Office, Patent # 19,063, January 5, 1858.

eventually superseded by the first can opener invented by Ezra Warner of Waterbury, Connecticut in 1858. Warner was issued U. S. Patent 19,053 on January 5, 1858. There would be improvements on Warner's basic design in future years, but his can opener was used during the Civil War and provided soldiers and civilians alike a reliable and safe method to open cans.

Consumer demand for tin cans spiked during the Civil War. Canned products were specialty items in the Civil War, not part of the regular Union Army ration. The United States government did purchase canned goods, but they were not issued to enlisted soldiers as part of their food allotment. Canned goods purchased by the government were resold to officer's messes, issued to soldiers of all ranks when hospitalized, or distributed when on assignment at a distant post where food supplies procured locally were precarious.

There were two other informal methods by which soldiers experienced canned food in the Civil War. Soldiers could purchase canned food from a semi-official person known as the regimental sutler. His mission was to provide the soldier what the army supply system did not, but at the soldier's personal expense. Another method outside of official Army distribution networks were packages sent from home. The packages, wooden shipping crates, were sent by family, friends, neighborhoods, and often entire local communities. Often these packages included expensive canned goods. By the end of the Civil War, nearly all soldiers had seen canned foods, and most had consumed them. Estimated annual canned food production in the United States slightly eclipsed 30 million by the end of the War, from 5 million at the beginning, and stoked a nationwide demand for more canned food products.

There were several types of tin cans offered for sale by canners to the public, but the predominant style of tin can in the nineteenth century was known as the "hole-in-cap" can. Also known as the "cap-hole" can, this style would dominate the industry until the early twentieth century. The can was comprised of four components: bottom, body, top, and cap. The body of the can was formed into a cylinder and soldered. The top and bottom were fitted on the outside of the body and soldered in place. The top had a 1 to 1½ inch opening cut in the center of the circular piece of tinplate. The food to be canned was thrust through this opening. The cap, slightly larger than the opening in the top, was soldered in place by an employee known as a "capper" once the food was inside the can.

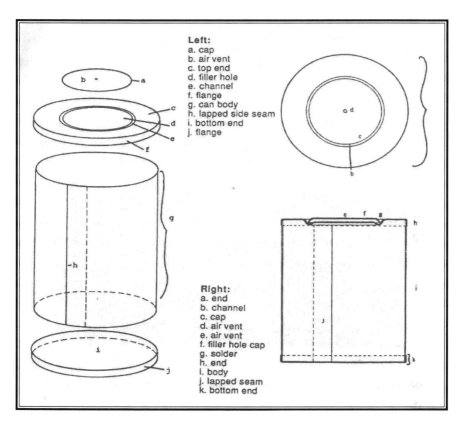

Left:
a. cap
b. air vent
c. top end
d. filler hole
e. channel
f. flange
g. can body
h. lapped side seam
i. bottom end
j. flange

Right:
a. end
b. channel
c. cap
d. air vent
e. air vent
f. filler hole cap
g. solder
h. end
i. body
j. lapped seam
k. bottom end

Hole-in-Cap Can: Adapted from Edward F. Heite, *Archaeological Data Recovery on the Collins, Geddes Cannery Site*, 14.

Post-Civil War

The "Golden Age" of technological development for tin cans was the four decades following the Civil War. The need, in the eyes of the canner and consumer, was lowering the price of canned goods so that they were amenable for mass consumption. Through the development of improved technology for the canning and can-making processes, the quest for lower prices was accomplished by the early twentieth century.

The first can-makers in America were tinsmiths who began making tin cans as part of their line of wares. "Craft or hand-made" can manufacturing was the first phase of technological development in can-making, characterized by extensive use of hand tools. An average tinsmith could make five or six cans per hour or 60 per day when working a ten-hour day. Hand tools were the predominant feature of early can-making, and mechanical innovations were limited until the late 1840s and early 1850s.

The second phase was "proto-mechanization," which began in the 1840s and lasted until the late 1860s. The developments in the phase concentrated on two distinct issues: expedited cutting of metal and quicker methods to solder side seams. Simple hand or foot-powered punch presses for tops and bottoms and slitters for cutting the bodies expedited the cutting of metal. Bench apparatus was also developed to rapidly solder these components together. By the mid-to-late1860s, after the impact of new methods for cutting metal and soldering the can together had diffused throughout the industry, can manufacturing rates were 60 cans per hour or 600 in a ten-hour work day. This was nearly a ten-fold improvement from craft practices.

The third phase was "semi-automatic mechanization" during which nearly every aspect of can manufacturing was transformed. Special attention in can-making was given to shearing tin plate, soldering side seams, and quicker soldering and attachment of tops and bottoms to cans. There were three distinguishing characteristics of this phase of can-making mechanization. First, these were individual machines designed to perform a mechanical operation for a specific step of the production process. Second, the power or motive force for these machines progressed from human hand or foot power to power from a variety of sources: water, steam, or coal gas. Finally, the capacity of can-making equipment increased dramatically. Can production rates demonstrated a significant leap forward during the semi-automatic phase of development when machinery was first introduced to can-making. The rates were highly dependent upon the type equipment employed by a can-maker, but rates of 1,500 per day were standard by 1880 and 2,500 per day by 1890. Rates of between 5,000 and 7,000 cans per day were possible, if several similar machines were used in conjunction with one another.

The fourth phase, "integration," began in the 1880s. The focus of integration was to link machines in a system of manufacture through a series of material handling devices, to optimize the entire system, rather than a single step in the can-making process, in order to form a continuous process line for the production of cans. The objectives in this phase were to reduce cost, decrease in-process inventory, facilitate continuous flow, and generate more throughput in can-making operations. Integration may have been imagined by can-makers and canners alike, but it burst upon the American canning industry unexpectedly in 1883. The individual responsible for developing the can assembly line was Edwin O. Norton of Chicago. Norton's line established the general layout and flow of machines and sequential functions for future can production lines. The Norton integrated can assembly line advertised rates of 3,000 cans an hour or 30,000 in a day.

The "Experimental" Sanitary Can

The tin can reached the final stage of development in the early twentieth century. This final stage of innovation, product design, altered the physical form of the tin can, as well as the production process. Known by several names: "open-top can," "The Ams Can," or most commonly "the sanitary can," this novel invention had its technological roots in an old tinsmiths' technique known as "double seaming." The double seam was a method by which tinsmiths joined two pieces of metal together without the use of solder. Each piece of metal had its edges rolled to form hooks, also referred to as flanges or curls. The hooks of each piece were rolled together forming a seam that consisted of five layers of metal. There were five individuals involved in developing the sanitary can: Max Ams and his son Charles, Julius Brenzinger, William Bogle, and George W. Cobb. Each played a specific role in the innovation process, yet only through their combined efforts did they successfully pioneer a solder-less can, one which is still recognizable today.

Max Ams had immigrated to New York from Germany during the

Civil War and opened a business, The Max Ams Company, selling a few canned goods such as apple butter and Russian caviar. Max and his son Charles developed a rubber gasket to seal the can. Charles was intrigued about the possibilities of rubber and in 1896 developed a rubber sealing material by dissolving rubber in a solution of ammonia and water. He believed his liquid rubber solution was an adequate sealant for the double seamed can, but he had yet to mechanize the process of applying the compound or develop a high-speed method for double seaming the ends.

In 1897, Ams hired engineer Julius Brenzinger to develop machinery for lining ends, drying them, and double seaming the ends onto cans. In 1898 he developed a machine, called a liner, for applying the Ams's rubber compound to the inside of the bent edge of an end, an area referred to by can-makers as the "curl." A few years later, he developed a double seamer specifically designed for the Ams rubber lined end. The terminology "sanitary can" was used to advertise that there was no solder used either inside or outside the can when attaching the ends, but it was still used outside the can to form the can body. However, the Ams Machine Company production was merely experimental; they were not producing the can in large quantities.

The commercialization of the "Ams Sanitary Can" depended upon the efforts of William Bogle and George Cobb. Bogle was a sales agent with offices on Park Place in New York City who possessed intimate knowledge of technological developments within the canning industry. He was a wholesale distributor of canned goods from various canners in New York and Pennsylvania. Bogle knew, by 1897, of the experiments of Max and Charles Ams with their revolutionary can. He convinced canner George Cobb, owner of the Cobb Preserving Company in Fairport, New York, to try the new can. Bogle believed the sanitary can was superior to the existing soldered can on the market as it was amenable to high-speed production, consumed less solder, and was more appealing to consumers because there was no possibility of solder mingling with food inside the can.

Sanitary Can. American Can Company Publication, circa 1930s.

The commercialization of the sanitary can by the Cobb Preserving Company was a classic application of experimentation and trial-and-error technological development. Cobb Preserving had to determine whether the new can was practical, how long they could sustain losses from their testing, and whether they could eliminate the spoilage generated by their experimentation. The initial test was in 1898, but the years 1899 through 1903 were the key years for commercial development of the sanitary can. Rather than buying small quantities of sanitary cans from the Max Ams Machine Company, Bogle and Cobb endeavored to make their own at Cobb's Fairport, New York cannery. Most of the cans they manufactured were for their own use, but they did sell the surplus to other canners whom Bogle thought might be interested in the new can. Progress was slow, costs were high, but according to Cobb "results each season were less disastrous." In 1902 William Bogle and Cobb's brother Frederick were quite frustrated and "ready to abandon the sanitary can." George "earnestly pleaded" for a final trial in 1903 and this season the results were "fairly successful," due to the assistance of redesigned machinery provided by the Max Ams Machine Company. In 1904, Cobb Preserving began exclusively making and packing the sanitary can in lieu of the hole-in-cap cans.

The painful years of trial-and-error development at Cobb Preserving were acutely experienced by those assigned to make and pack the cans. John Rees was an employee of Cobb Preserving who spent summers during college working in the factory. He noted that there were many problems with the development of the can, particularly cans swelling and bursting from over pressurization during canning. Cobb Preserving overcame this problem by trail-and-error, experimenting with various temperatures and cooking times for the contents of the can, until they had fairly reliable pressure cooking guidelines for nearly all the fruits and vegetables packed. According to Rees, "year after year it [the sanitary can] became more effective and it got to a period where we felt pretty secure with our work with pressure cans."

Roy Wheeler was another can-maker at Cobb Preserving and was moved to the development work on the sanitary can. The initial experiments were so calamitous, Wheeler declared, "I know from my experience in making these open top cans that so many poor ones were made that we filled the canal [Erie Canal] with them. That was during the experimental days." The manufacturing problems encountered by Wheeler were primarily the accumulation of solder at the ends of the side seam which made double seaming difficult. Wheeler and his compatriots overcame these production issues by soldering the can cylinders horizontally, rather than vertically. Wheeler believed that the sanitary can was so much easier to manufacture, that can-makers had no cause for complaint. It was a practical innovation, in his observation, and a great benefit for canners.

Ams, Bogle, and George Cobb were so convinced and enthusiastic with the successful development at Cobb Preserving, and commercial possibilities of the sanitary can, that they formed a separate company for commercializing the can in 1904. The firm was named the Sanitary Can Company (SCC) and began making cans in July 1904. Initial sales of the sanitary can were so promising, that SCC had to assume large amounts of debt to finance their expansion. A nationwide financial downturn in 1907 prompted the officers of SCC to sell their company to the American Can Company in 1908. With the largest can manufacturing company in America behind the sanitary can, sales exploded. By the early 1920s, the "hole-in-cap" can was virtually extinct, and the sanitary can had been adopted by nearly all canners. Sales of all tin food cans in 1923 was 2.3 billion. In the space of less than 20 years, the sanitary can had progressed from a novel experiment with sales of almost nothing, to the standard can for the entire industry. Experimentation and the belief and drive of its innovators were the reasons for its success.

Lessons Learned

Despite contemporary nostalgic hagiography about innovators such as Fred Smith, Steve Jobs, and Elon Musk, the era of the independent inventor vanished in the 1920s. Research and development post-World War I became systematized and centered in industrial research laboratories of large commercial companies. The same was true of the can-making industry. The duopoly formed by American Can Company and the Continental Can Company controlled nearly 80 percent of the can manufacturing market, and the research activities of the industry were positioned within their internal organizational structure. Experimentation remained an important development activity, however, but the boundaries and latitude allowed researchers became more constrained, primarily because of financial risk.

The story of the tin can industry illustrates several important characteristics of experimentation. First, hedge risk with small bets. Many of the early innovators in the industry were severely financially constrained, so improved machinery during the mechanization of the industry were often incremental improvements on existing designs. Also, the sanitary can was such a novel, yet chancy proposition, that most canners only risked a small portion of their packed goods to the new can. However, once it had satisfied their expectations, they quickly committed more goods to the new style can. Second, the development and commercialization of the sanitary can demonstrates the importance of a multi-functional development team. Ams and Brenzinger were engineers, Cobb an expert in operational matters, and Bogle the financier, salesman, and promoter of the sanitary can. Absent any of these individuals, the development of the sanitary can may have taken a much different path. Third, during experimentation an end point or prior determination on when to stop experimenting if the desired results are not obtained, at least for the time being, must be established. Cobb Preserving was at this point in 1902 when they had yet to perfect the sanitary can and were absorbing tremendous financial expense. However, the belief in the sanitary can's utility convinced the project team to make 1903 their final year of development and eventually they perfected their design and processing equipment within the year. Finally, in experimentation there is a trade-off between risk and reward. The case of Cobb Preserving demonstrates a company taking extreme risks, but the reward was a transformational product which completely dominated an industry within less than 20 years.

CONCLUSION

I n an environment of volatility, uncertainty, complexity and ambiguity, organizations cannot guarantee a positive strategic outcome. Perceptive Leaders recognize that they can raise the probability of a good outcome by focusing on two levers: their own skills in decision making and their ability to manage the uncertainty.

In this handbook, we illustrated organizational capabilities and leadership behaviors that strengthen these levers. We also provided concrete actions to support these competencies, which are included in the text of each chapter. Finally, we offered some common language phrases a Perceptive Leader can adopt to reinforce these organizational competencies. We provide here a final summary chart as a reference.

PERCEPTIVE LEADERSHIP

	Chapter	Leadership Behaviors	Common Language
P	Purpose	Ensure clarity on the overall strategic purpose or intent.	Commander's Intent
E	Experiential Frames	Seek diversity of thought.	Diversity of Thought
R	Range of Alternatives	Develop many alternatives.	Overconfidence Bias
C	Contrary Views	Seek opposing views.	Devil's Advocate
E	External Landscape	Distinguish between forces for which you know the outcome and forces for which the outcome is unknown.	Trends and Uncertainties
P	Productive Paranoia	Challenge the organizational assumptions.	Organizational Mental Model
T	Trust	Create an environment that supports transparency.	Radical Candor
I	Internal Conditions	Build a culture that encourages adaptability.	Culture of Agility
V	Vigilance	Pay attention to leading indicators of changes in the external environment.	Weak Signals
E	Experimentation	Encourage small bets to learn about uncertainties, customers, external environment generally.	Test and Learn

We provide one final story, to illustrate how this handbook has been a learning journey for us as well. We think of this work as a small bet, or rapid (maybe NOT-so-rapid) experiment. For example, we may one day expand the handbook into a more detailed book with deeper research and anecdotes.

And of course, we have learned a great deal about how easy it is to "preach" and not so easy to "do." As we were choosing a cover for the book, we used a crowdsourcing approach, because we were spotting early indicators that the publishing industry is adopting these practices. We received over 55 different designs from across the world, and we chose the winner based on its simplicity and emphasis on uncertainty, or luck.

We both showed the chosen cover to family and friends, and Kathy began to include the cover in her slide deck when addressing various executive groups. After showing the cover to probably 250 people, Kathy was speaking to a group of approximately 100 securities leaders at The Wharton School. The cover she shared is below:

An audience member raised his hand and said, "I assume you *meant* to have two two's on one dice?" Kathy hesitated, horrified, because of course *no one* had mentioned this, and we certainly had not noticed. She quickly recovered and responded, "How perceptive of you!"

We debated whether to keep the flawed cover or correct the dice photo. After all, we had just written a handbook on Perceptive Leadership! In the end, we decided to replace the photo. However, the dice served to illustrate how, even in the most mundane of circumstances, our brains default to what we have seen in the past, and we inevitably ignore what does not fit into our experiential frames.

Best of luck spotting the two two's on your dice!

BIBLIOGRAPHY

Introduction

Duke, Annie. *Thinking in Bets: Making Smarter Decisions When You Don't Have All the Facts*. New York: Penguin Random House, 2018.

Fournier, Susan. "Introducing New Coke." *Harvard Business School Case*, HBS Case 500067-PDF-ENG, December 17, 1999.

Lovallo, Dan and Oliver Sibony. "The Case for Behavioral Strategy." *McKinsey Quarterly*, March 2010.

Chapter 1—Purpose

Ambrose, Stephen E. *D-Day June 6, 1944: The Climactic Battle of World War II*. New York: Simon & Schuster, 1994.

Hastings, Max. *Overlord: D-Day and the Battle for Normandy*. New York: Random House, 1984.

Hrebiniak, Lawrence G. *Making Strategy Work: Leading Effective Execution and Change*. 2nd ed., New York: Pearson Education, Inc., 2013.

Sull, Donald, Rebecca Homkes and Charles Sull. "Why Strategy Execution Unravels and What to Do About It." Harvard *Business Review*, R1503C-PDF-ENG, March 15, 2015.

Chapter 2—Experiential Frames

Collins, Jim and Morten T. Hansen. *Great by Choice: Uncertainty, Chaos, and Luck— Why Some Thrive Despite Them All*. New York: Harper Collins Books, 2011.

Kahneman, Daniel and Amos Tversky. "Prospect Theory: An Analysis of Decision Under Risk." *Econometrica,* Vol. 47, No. 2 (March 1979): 263-292.

Grant, Ulysses S. *Personal Memoirs*. New York: The Modern Library, 1999 [1885].

Goodwin, Doris Kearns. *Team of Rivals: The Political Genius of Abraham Lincoln*. New York: Simon and Schuster Paperbacks, 2006.

Lewis, Allison and David Reynolds. "Teams Solve Problems Faster When They Are More Cognitively Diverse." *Harvard Business Review*, H03IBV-PDF-ENG, March 30, 2017.

Lorenzo, Rocio, Nicole Voight, Miki Tsusaka, Matt Krentz, and Katie Abouzhar. "How Diverse Leadership Teams Boost Innovation." Boston: The Boston Consulting Group, January 23, 2018.

Rosen, Rebecca. "The Q Score: How Y Combinator's Startups Are Like Broadway Musicals." *The Atlantic*, March 14, 2012.

Chapter 3—Range of Alternatives

Heath, Chip and Dan Heath. *Decisive: How to Make Better Choices in Life and Work.* New York: Crown Business Books, 2013.

Hughes, Thomas P. *American Genesis: A Century of Invention and Technological Enthusiasm, 1870-1970.* Chicago: The University of Chicago Press, 1989.

Nye, David E. *Electrifying America: Social Meanings of a New Technology.* Cambridge, Mass.: The MIT Press, 1992.

Shefrin, Hersh and Enrico Maria Cervellati. "BP's Failure to Debias." *Quarterly Journal of Finance, Vol. 1, No. 1 (January 2011): 127-168.*

Chapter 4—Contrary Views

De Bono, Edward. *Six Thinking Hats.* New York: MICA Management Resources, 1999.

Klein, Gary. "Performing a Project Pre-Mortem." *IEEE Engineering Management Review*, Vol. 36, No. 2 (June 2008): 103-104.

Gaddis, John Lewis. *We Now Know: Rethinking Cold War History.* New York: Oxford University Press, 1997.

Hart, William, Dolores Albarracin, Alice H. Eagly, Inge Brechan, Matthew J. Lindberg, and Lisa Merrill. "Feeling Validated Versus Being Correct: A Meta-Analysis of Selective Exposure to Information." *Psychological Bulletin*, Vol. 134, No. 4 (July 2009): 555-588.

Janis, Irving L. *Groupthink: Psychological Studies of Policy Decisions and Fiascoes.* Boston: Wadsworth Cengage Learning, 1982.

Chapter 5—External Landscape

Lengel, Edward G. *General George Washington: A Military Life.* New York: Random House, 2005.

Morris, James M. *America's Armed Forces: A History.* 2nd ed., Upper Saddle River, New Jersey: Prentice Hall, 1996.

Rumsfeld, Donald. *Department of Defense News Briefing*, February 12, 2002.

Taleb, Nassim Nicholas. *The Black Swan: The Impact of the Highly Improbable.* New York: Random House, 2007.

Fooled By Randomness: The Hidden Role of Chance in Life and the Markets. New York: Random House, 2004.

Chapter 6—Productive Paranoia

Collins, Jim and Morten T. Hansen. *Great by Choice: Uncertainty, Chaos, and Luck— Why Some Thrive Despite Them All.* New York: Harper Collins Books, 2011.

The Guardian (London). October 20, 2015.

Wall Street Journal (New York). April 12, 2012; July 31, 2013; April 18, 2014; June 23, 2015; July 30, 2015; October 7, 2015; December 17, 2015; April 15, 2017.

Chapter 7—Trust

Covey, Stephen M. R. and Rebecca R. Merrill. *The Speed of Trust*. New York: Free Press, 2006.

Grant, Ulysses S. *Personal Memoirs*. New York: The Modern Library, 1999 [1885].

Goodwin, Doris Kearns. *Team of Rivals: The Political Genius of Abraham Lincoln*. New York: Simon and Schuster Paperbacks, 2006.

Langley, Monica. "Inside Mulally's 'War Room': A Radical Overhaul of Ford." *Wall Street Journal* (New York), December 22, 2006.

Lencioni, Patrick. *Overcoming the Five Dysfunctions of a Team*. New York: Jossey-Bass, 2005.

Scott, Kim. *Radical Candor: Be a Kick-Ass Boss Without Losing Your Humanity*. New York: St. Martin's Press, 2017.

Chapter 8—Internal Conditions

Berlin, Leslie. *The Man Behind the Microchip: Robert Noyce and the Invention of Silicon Valley*. New York: Oxford University Press, 2005.

Groysberg, Boris, Jeremiah Lee, Jesse Price, and Yo-Jud Cheng. "The Leader's Guide to Corporate Culture." *Harvard Business Review*, R1801B-PDF-ENG, January 1, 2018.

Nadler, David A. and Michael L. Tushman. *Competing by Design: The Power of Organizational Architecture*. New York: Oxford University Press, 1997.

Malone, Michael S. *The Intel Trinity: How Robert Noyce, Gordon Moore, and Andy Grove Built the World's Most Important Company*. New York: Harper Collins, 2014.

McChrystal, Stanley. *Team of Teams: New Rules of Engagement in a Complex World*. New York: Penguin Publishing Group, 2015.

Sull, Donald, Rebecca Homkes and Charles Sull. "Why Strategy Execution Unravels and What to Do About It." *Harvard Business Review*, R1503C-PDF-ENG, March 15, 2015.

Teitleman, Robert. *Profits of Science: The American Marriage of Business and Technology*. New York: Basic Books, 1994.

Chapter 9—Vigilance

Gino, Francesca, Todd B. Kashdan, David J. Disabato, Fallon R. Goodman, Carl NaughtonClaudio Fernandez-Araoz, Andrew Roscoe, and Kentaro Aramaki. "The Business Case for Curiosity." *Harvard Business Review*, R1805B-PDF-ENG, September 1, 2018.

Berlin, Leslie. *The Man Behind the Microchip: Robert Noyce and the Invention of Silicon Valley*. New York: Oxford University Press, 2005.

Malone, Michael S. *The Intel Trinity: How Robert Noyce, Gordon Moore, and Andy Grove Built the World's Most Important Company*. New York: Harper Collins, 2014.

Teitleman, Robert. *Profits of Science: The American Marriage of Business and Technology*. New York: Basic Books, 1994.

Chapter 10—Experimentation

Christiansen, Clayton. *The Innovator's Dilemma*. Boston: Harvard Business School Publishing, 1997.

Liker, Jeffrey. *The Toyota Way: 14 Management Principles from the World's Greatest Manufacturer*. New York: McGraw-Hill, 2003.

McChrystal, Stanley. *Team of Teams: New Rules of Engagement in a Complex World*. New York: Penguin Publishing Group, 2015.

Pearson, Gregg S. "The Democratization of Food: Tin Cans and the Growth of the American Food Processing Industry, 1810-1940." Ph.D. diss., Lehigh University, 2016.

Wladawsky-Berger, Irving. "Fostering an Innovation Culture: Talent, Discipline and Leadership." *The Wall Street Journal* (New York), March 2, 2019.

PHOTO SOURCES

Chapter 1

1.1 and 1.2 Pointe-du-Hoc photos attributed to Gregg Pearson, 2006.

1.3 Colonel James Earl Rudder photo attributed to U.S. Army and *www.benning.army.*

1.4 and 1.5 Pointe-du-Hoc photos attributed to Gregg Pearson, 2006.

Chapter 2

2.1 Lincoln and his Cabinet attributed to *Alamy.com.*

Chapter 3

3.1 Thomas Edison photo attributed to *Alamy.com.*

3.2 Nikola Tesla photo attributed to *Alamy.com.*

3.3 First electric chair photo attributed to *Alamy.com.*

Chapter 4

4.1 Reconnaissance photo attributed to Getty Images.

Chapter 5

5.1 George Washington painting photo attributed to painting by John Trumbull, 1792 on Wikipedia.

Chapter 6

6.1 King C Gillette photo attributed to Wikipedia, found 2019, photo circa 1910.

6.2 Gillette Safety Razor photo attributed to *Alamy.com.*

Chapter 10

10. 1 Diagram of Ezra Warner's Can Opener attributed to U. S. Patent and Trademark Office, Patent # 19,063, January 5, 1858.

10.2 Hole-in-Cap Can photo attributed to Edward F. Heite, *Archaeological Data Recovery on the Collins, Geddes Cannery Site*, 14.

10. 3 Sanitary Can photo attributed to *American Can Company Publication*, circa 1930s.

Made in the USA
Monee, IL
25 June 2021